History 13-16 Project

D1635651

Conflict In Ireland

Tony McAleavy

General Editor: Aileen Plummer

Collins Educational
An imprint of HarperCollins*Publishers*

First published in 1987 by Holmes McDougall under the aegis of the School Curriculum
Development Committee

Further information on the History (13-16) Project can be obtained from The Director, Schools History Project (13-16), Trinity and All Saints College, Brownberrie Lane, Leeds LS18 5HD.

Illustrations by Denby Designs, John F. Martin and David Wilson

Cover Picture by permission of Pacemaker Press

First published in 1987 in Holmes McDougall Ltd, Edinburgh

This edition published 1991 by Collins Educational, An *imprint of* HarperCollins*Publishers*
77-85 Fulham Palace Road, London W6 8JB

Reprinted 1993, 1994 (twice), 1995

ISBN 0 00 325100 4

Produced in Hong Kong

Contents

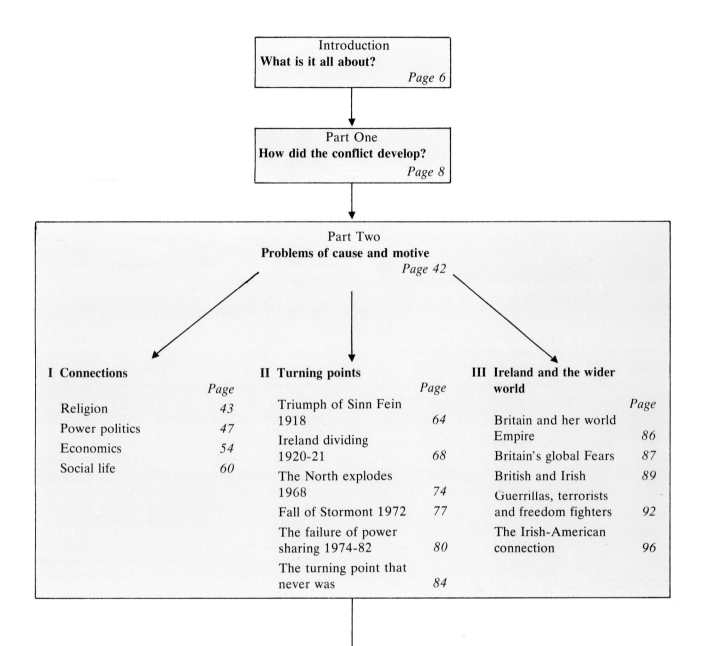

Conflict in Ireland

A   Riot police in Ulster 1969.

B   Riot police in Ulster 1886.

If you have been watching television news recently you will probably have seen pictures like A and E But if you had been reading a newspaper 100 years ago, you could have seen similar pictures like B and D This is because the same conflict was going on then.

In fact, people have been fighting and suffering for over 300 years as part of a violent argument about Ireland's future and Ireland's past. As in most conflicts, the people involved have been not just soldiers and police but ordinary people, just like you.

In this book we shall be looking at four key questions about today's conflict in Ulster:

▶ *What is it about?*
▶ *Why did it develop?*
▶ *What has the conflict got to do with the wider world?*
▶ *What happens next?*

C   An IRA sniper 1970s.

SOURCE 1 — Children of the conflict

The 'Eve of the Twelfth of July' (1970) was a quiet day in the Catholic area. The 12th was the Protestants' day of celebration and remembrance. It commemorated the Battle of the Boyne in 1690 where the Protestant forces of King William of Orange defeated the Catholics under the command of James II. Every child knew the story . . .

'I think I'll take a wee walk', said Kevin. They fell into line. Kate linked arms with Brede. Kevin and Brian walked a little apart. They turned into the main road. There, on the opposite pavement, were Sadie and her brother Tommy and several other children.

This is what they had been waiting for all week: to stand face to face, Catholic and Protestant, with only a strip of road separating them. The moment of quiet passed. Now the voices were raised, soft and taunting to begin with . . .

'Dirty Micks!'

'Filthy ould Prods!'

Tempers flared. The voices grew louder.

'Kick the Pope!'

'To hell with King Billy!'

No one knew who threw the first stone. One seemed to come from each side simultaneously. It was as if a whistle has been blown. Suddenly children came swarming out of the side streets, yelling and cheering, booing. Their hands scoured the ground for any ammunition they could find: pieces of wood, half bricks . . .

(adapted from 'The Twelfth Day of July' a story by Joan Lingard, 1970)

D   Political murder in Dublin 1882.

E   Political murder in Dublin 1976.

F   Protestant propaganda showing Catholic rebels roasting children alive 1641.

G   Catholic children starving in the Great Famine 1846.

H   Catholic boy with a home-made petrol bomb 1969.

▶ *Look at the pictures and source 1. How have children and young people been affected by the conflict over the centuries?*

▶ *How do you think the involvement of children has helped to keep the conflict alive?*

▶ *What problems of bias and reliability can you spot in these sources?*

What is it all about?

Today Ireland is divided into two parts:

The North sometimes called Ulster is part of the United Kingdom. This means that it is ruled by the British Parliament in London and has the Queen as head of state.

The South is an independent country with its own government and parliament in Dublin. A President is head of state. It is called The Republic of Ireland.

The recent violence in Ireland is all about one simple question:

Should the North stay part of the UK or should it join the South as part of a united and independent Ireland?

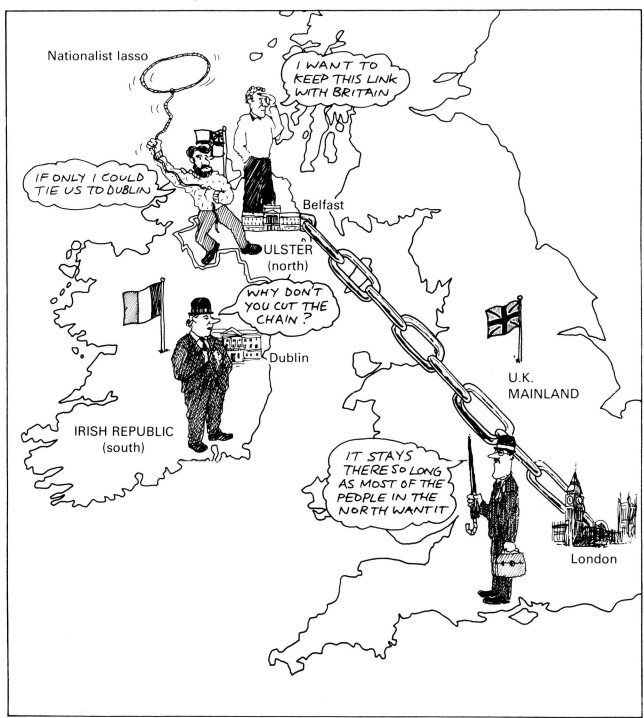

One simple question — should Northern Ireland stay in the UK?

This question has resulted in conflict for three main reasons:

1. The people of the North cannot agree about the answer.

One side want to stay part of the UK. They are called Unionists or Loyalists. They are mostly Protestants.

The other side want the North to join the South and become part of the Irish Republic. They are called Nationalists or Republicans. They are mostly Catholics.

2. Both sides have private armies willing to use the bullet rather than the ballot to solve the problem.

Although most Irish people do not support the use of violence, these private armies are preventing a peaceful solution to the conflict.

3. The governments of the UK and the Irish Republic cannot agree about their answers.

Their exact attitude varies from time to time, depending on the political party in power but since 1969 each has stuck to the same general line.

The British government has said that it will not withdraw from Northern Ireland unless or until a majority of the people there agree to this.

Look at the graphs.
▶ *Which side is in the majority in Northern Ireland: Unionists or Nationalists?*
▶ *Which side would be in a majority in the whole of Ireland?*
▶ *Who ought to have a say in the decision about the future of Northern Ireland?*

Northern Ireland, Voting patterns in the 1987 General Election

All Ireland population, 1981 = 4.89 million

The British Isles, 1981 population = 59.2 million

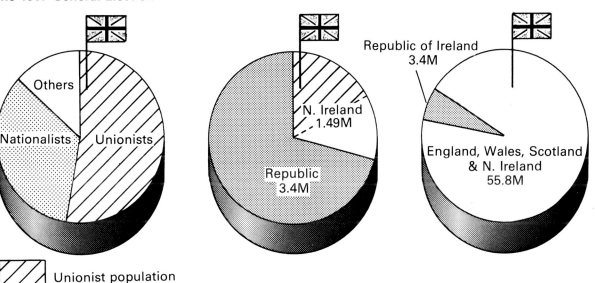

Unionist population

Population and politics — which majority should decide on the future of Northern Ireland?

Before we ask why there is a conflict in Ireland today, we first have to know how this conflict developed. In the introduction we say how today's conflict centres around:

1. A divided Ireland and the future of the North.

2. The hopes and fears of the main groups involved.

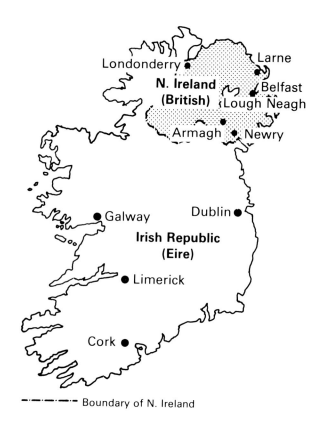

Divided Ireland.

But is this how things have always been?
▶ *Has Ireland always been divided into two separate states: North and South?*
▶ *Have the people in the North always been divided into opposite groups: Unionists and Nationalists; Protestants and Catholics?*
▶ *Have the British always controlled part of Ireland?*

If you look at the timeline you can find a short answer to these questions:

▶ *When did these splits first happen?*
▶ *When did the British first become involved in Ireland?*

Timeline — The main stages of Irish History 100BC to present

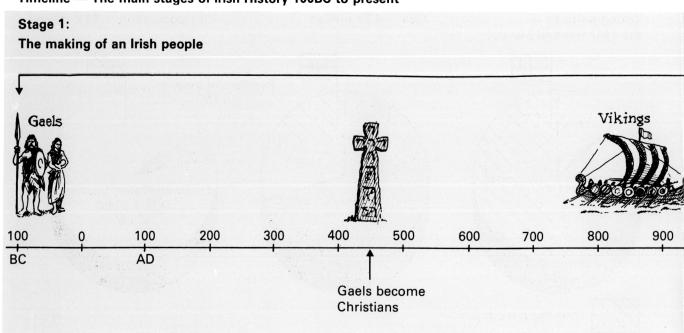

Stage 1:
The making of an Irish people

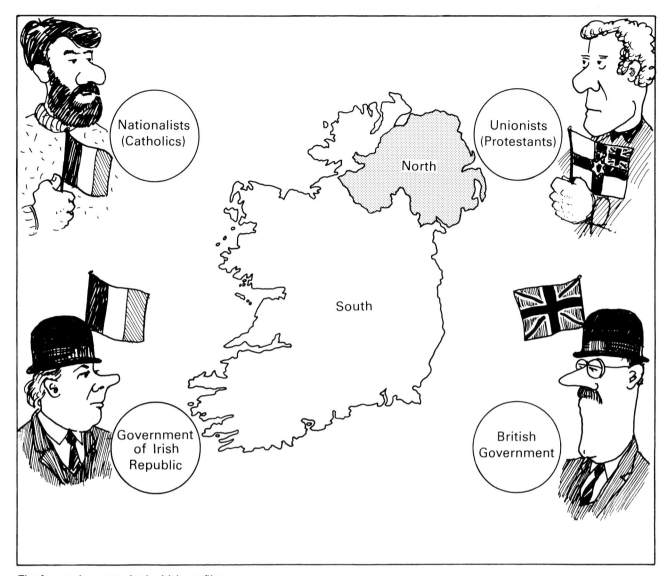

The four main groups in the Irish conflict.

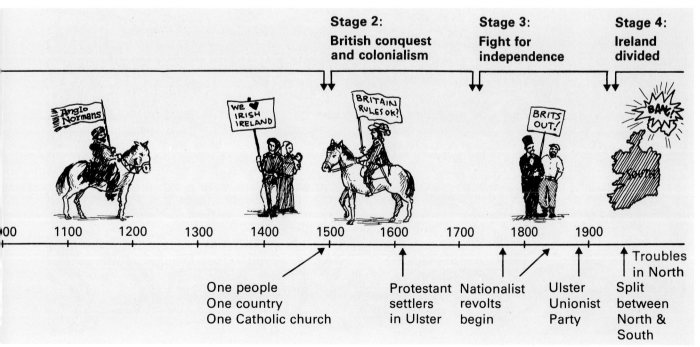

A short history of the Irish Conflict

Stage 1　Making an Irish people 100 BC - 1500 AD

Between 100 BC - 1500 AD three groups of settlers came to Ireland: Gaels, Vikings and Norman-English knights.

→

Although this led to conflict, in time they all merged into a single Irish people.

→

By 1500 the Irish people followed the Gaelic way of life and the Catholic faith.

Stage 2　British conquest and colonisation 1500-1790

In the 16th century English Protestant rulers decided to take control of Ireland.

→

They took land from the Catholic Irish and gave it to Protestant settlers from England and Scotland.

→

By 1690 these Protestant settlers controlled the land and government of Ireland for the English kings.

Stage 3 The fight for Irish Independence

After 1790, two groups of Irish people began a struggle to free Ireland from British rule. They were called NATIONALISTS.

1790-1914 Revolutionary Nationalists tried to win complete independence by revolts and rebellions. These all failed.

1820-1914 Parliamentary Nationalists tried to win a separate Irish parliament by peaceful persuasion.

1790-1914 Irish Protestants, especially in the North, decided to fight to keep Ireland and Britain united. They were called UNIONISTS.

By 1914 it seemed that the Parliamentary Nationalists had forced the British Government to give Ireland a separate parliament. World War I stopped this happening.

→

After the war, in the 1918 election, the Revolutionary Nationalists won a surprise victory. They set up their own government in Dublin.

→

During a fierce guerrilla war 1919-21, British rule collapsed in much of Ireland — but not in Ulster. Here Unionists continued to oppose a break with Britain.

Stage 4   Ireland divided 1920-1987

North and South 1920-1968

Since 1920-1 Ireland has been divided into two parts, North and South. The South became an independent country with a largely Catholic government.

→

The North has stayed part of Britain. Protestant Unionists have controlled the government.

→

Catholic Nationalists in the North were treated unfairly by the Protestant Unionists.

The troubles in the North 1968-87

In 1968 trouble broke out in the North between Protestant Unionists and Catholic Nationalists.

→

In 1969 the British government sent in troops to keep order. In 1972 they took power from the Protestants and began direct rule from Britain.

→

Since 1971 the IRA have killed hundreds of soldiers and police. Protestant Unionist gangs have also carried out many killings.

1 Making an Irish people 100 BC-1500 AD

In 1972 Paul McCartney wrote a song about 'The Troubles' in Ireland today. His solution was that Britain should 'Give Ireland back to the Irish'.

▶ *But who are the Irish?*
▶ *When did they first become 'one people'?*
▶ *When did the British take over their country?*

The people who live in Ireland today are all descended from the many different groups of invaders who crossed over to Ireland from Britain or the continent of Europe.

The coming of the Gaels

The first settlers arrived during the Stone Age, around 9,000 BC. From the first century BC onwards, Gaelic people invaded Ireland. Over the next 400 years they gradually took control of the country. They imposed their language and laws on the people and, in time, intermarried with them. They did not make Ireland into one single kingdom, however. The country was divided into a series of small kingdoms grouped into four provinces: Ulster, Leinster, Munster and Connacht.

The Gaelic invasion made a lasting impression on Ireland. A version of the language spoken by the Gaels is still used for everyday speech in parts of western Ireland. The language is now called 'Irish' and it is taught in most Catholic schools.

THE COMING OF FINN

Finn MacCool and his Fenians were a band of brave warriors in ancient Gaelic legends. Like King Arthur's Knights they were sworn to fight for justice. In the nineteenth century a group of Irish nationalists, who wanted to throw the British out of Ireland by force, called themselves "The Fenians". Why do you think they did so?

In the 5th century the Gaels became Christians and religion has been a powerful influence on Irish life ever since. According to ancient tradition, Christianity was brought by St. Patrick. In fact this most 'Irish' of historical figures was another immigrant — probably from the west coast of Britain.

Between 500-800 AD Gaelic Ireland became one of the most important centres of learning in Europe. Irish scholars and missionaries travelled across Europe setting up schools and monasteries.

Today Irish nationalists are very proud of their Gaelic past because they feel it clearly sets them apart from the British. They look back on this 'golden age' as proof of what Irish people could do if only they were free of foreign interference.

The mid-7th century Book of Durrow — a product of the Gaelic Golden age.

SOURCE 1 — Looking back to the 'golden age'

I believe that it is our Gaelic past which is at the bottom of our heart. We must never forget that the Ireland of today is the descendant of 7th century Ireland. The failure of Irish people in recent times is due to our ceasing to be Irish without becoming English.

(Douglas Hyde, founder of the Gaelic League, 1894)

The Viking and Norman invasions

This 'golden age' came to a sudden end with two new invasions. From around 800 AD groups of Vikings began to arrive in Ireland. They were followed in 1167 by Norman knights who crossed over to Ireland around 100 years after the Norman conquest of Britain. Both groups of invaders threatened the way of life of Ireland's Gaelic chiefs and their people. The Vikings were pagans. The Normans owed loyalty to a king across the sea. In 1171 their king, Henry II of England, visited them and decided to call himself 'Lord of Ireland'.

As things turned out, these newcomers made very few changes. In time both groups intermarried with the Irish. The Vikings became Christians and set themselves up as traders in towns along the coast. The Normans learned to live like Gaelic chiefs. The kings of England hardly ever visited the country and had little influence except in a small area around Dublin, known as 'the Pale'.

A Norman knight in Ireland — one in a long line of invaders.

SOURCE 2 — Going native, 1336

While at the time of the conquest the invaders spoke their own language, now many of them have abandoned this and their way of life. Instead they use the customs and language of the Irish. They have married and allied themselves with the King's Irish enemies.

(Adapted from the 'Laws of Kilkenny' which tried to stop Norman settlers mixing with native Irish people)

Ireland in 1500

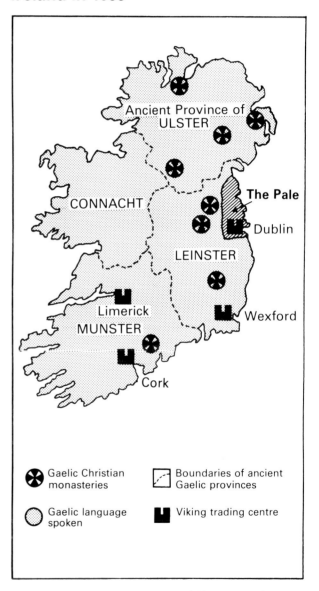

Ireland in 1500: One language, one faith, one people.

By 1500 the power of the English kings over Irish life 'beyond the Pale' had dwindled to virtually nothing. The situation in Ireland was not really very different from that in 800. Ireland remained divided into a series of small kingdoms (some of them now ruled by Norman Irish families) but its people shared the same language and religion.

2 British conquests and colonisation

In the 16th century there was an important change in the relationship between the English and the Irish. English rulers began to take a closer interest in Ireland. This was mainly because they feared Ireland could become a threat to their own power.

For centuries there had been political quarrels between the kings of Europe. Now there were religious quarrels too. By 1560 England had cut all links with the Roman Catholic Church and England became a Protestant country. Ireland, however, remained staunchly Catholic and there was a real danger that Ireland would be used as a base to attack England by her Catholic enemies in Europe. The English rulers decided the time had come to take firm control of Ireland and its people.

▶ *What effects did this decision have?*

Tudor expeditions

Henry VIII made the first moves in a long campaign to make the Irish loyal Protestant subjects of their English king. In 1541 he changed his title from 'Lord' to 'King of Ireland' and told the Irish chieftains they were all responsible to him.

His successors, Edward VI and Elizabeth I, encouraged English settlers to go and live in Ireland. They also began introducing Protestant bishops, bibles and prayer books. But most Irish people refused to accept the English religion or English rule. In Elizabeth's reign, the provinces of Ulster and Munster rose in rebellion led by their noble families. Elizabeth sent her armies to defeat the rebels. This they did, treating the survivors with ruthless cruelty.

Irish chieftains fighting, an English view 1581.

SOURCE 1 — The people of Munster after the 1581 rebellion

Out of every corner of the woods they came, creeping forth on their hands for their legs would not bear them. They looked like skeletons; they ate corpses. If they found a plot of shamrocks, they flocked there as a feast.

(written by Edmund Spenser, an English official in Munster, 1583)

The Protestant plantations

In the 17th century English rulers decided that military force was not the best way to gain control in Ireland. Land was still the main source of power. As long as the land in Ireland stayed in the hands of Catholic nobles, they would still be able to raise the men, horses and supplies to rebel. So the English kings decided to try a different approach. They would 'plant' colonies of loyal Protestants and give land to them. This idea was not new. It had been tried in the 16th century but all these early settlements had failed. This time the English government had to make sure the settlements, or 'plantations' had enough people and money to survive and grow.

There were many plantations across Ireland but the most important was in Ulster — the province which had rebelled against Elizabeth I. From 1610 onwards,

The coming of the Protestants: the Tudor and Stuart Plantations.

thousands of Protestants came over to Ulster and settled on land taken from local Irish Catholics. Some of them were English Anglicans (supporters of the Church of England). Others were Scottish Protestants or dissenters. They disagreed with Anglican ways but were still loyal to the king.

Catholic rebellion

The Catholics of Ulster felt angry and cheated by the plantations. In 1641 they took part in a great rebellion against the new settlers. Large numbers of Protestants were killed and the rebellion continued till the arrival of the English leader, Oliver Cromwell, in 1649. Cromwell was determined to teach the Irish Catholics a lesson. He did this by slaughtering the Catholic inhabitants of two towns, Drogheda and Wexford. Afterwards he confiscated the lands of the Catholic rebels and drove them into the poor Western province of Connacht. The rebellion was over but it has never been forgotten. For centuries afterwards Protestants in Ulster feared attacks. Catholics today still talk about the cruelties of Cromwell.

SOURCE 2 — Memories of the 1641 rebellion

A Protestant artist's view, 1640s

The massacre of Portadown Bridge 1641.

A historian's view, 1983
The outbreak of the rebellion in 1641 had been marked by the massacre or death from starvation of about 12,000 Scottish and English planters. This was not part of a deliberate plan. Many times Catholic priests intervened to save planters' lives.

(John Ranelagh, 'A Short History of Ireland', 1983)

A Protestant politician's view, 1969

In 1641 the Roman Catholic Church decided to exterminate the Protestants in Ulster and there took place one of the most bloody massacres in Irish history. It was led by the priests of the Roman Catholics and the rivers of Ulster ran red with Protestant blood. The River Bann was so choked with Protestant bodies, that the Roman Catholics could walk dry-shod across the river.

(Ian Paisley, September 1969)

▶ *How do these sources differ?*
▶ *How do you explain the differences?*

The Ulster Plantation: a turning point

The plantation of Ulster was the first important turning point along the road to today's conflict in Ireland. Unlike earlier invaders, these new settlers did not intermarry with the old Irish families. Instead they kept their Protestant religion and their English language. They despised and feared the native Irish and kept themselves separate as much as possible. They remained loyal to their rulers across the sea and to their Protestant religion. In return, they expected British Protestants to help them against the Irish. As we have seen, though Ireland had long been divided into separate provinces, her people had shared the same religion and way of life. Now, from the 17th century onwards, there were two separate hostile 'communities' in Ulster: the descendants of the Protestant British settlers and the native Irish Catholics. From the beginning, their differences were not just about religion but also about political and economic power. As Protestant settlers increased their hold on land and power, so the native Catholics steadily lost it. This 'tug-of-war' is still at the root of today's problems.

SOURCE 3 — Modern Protestants look back to the Plantations

The idea that Ireland must be ruled as one unit is totally false. Northern Ireland is utterly different from the Republic of Ireland. This reality has existed for 400 years. It dates from 'The Ulster Plantation' in the early years of the 17th century. These settlers brought with them a way of life which was totally different to that in the rest of Ireland. From that moment the Province of Ulster developed its own way of life. To this day this difference continues.

('Irish Unification — Never' a pamphlet by the Democratic Unionist Party, 1984)

The Protestant takeover (1690-1770)

Despite Cromwell's victory the Protestants' hold on power in Ireland was not yet firm. When Catholic James II became King in 1685, the Irish Protestants began to fear that their land — and their power — would be given back to the Catholics. Even when James was expelled from the English throne in 1688, their position was not safe. Within a year James had landed in Ireland with an army of French troops. He planned to use Ireland as a base to invade England to regain his throne. This was the kind of situation English rulers had feared since the time of the Spanish Armada.

The battle of the Boyne 1690: a turning point

The hopes of James and the Irish Catholics were dashed in 1690. The new King, William of Orange, followed James to Ireland with his own army and defeated him at the Battle of the Boyne on July 1st 1690. William of Orange's victory marked a second turning point along the road to today's conflict. After 1690 Protestants made sure they had complete control of Ireland. Ulster Protestants still celebrate the Battle of the Boyne today.

Protestants prevented any further attempts by Catholics to regain power. More Catholic land was confiscated so that by 1703 Catholics held only 14% of the land in Ireland. Since the right to vote was linked to land ownership the Irish Parliament was now controlled by Protestants — mainly Anglican landlords.

The Penal Laws

Between 1697 and 1727 the Irish Parliament passed special laws known as The Penal Laws. They remained in force till the end of the 18th century. The chart shows what effect these had on Catholics.

The Anglican ruling class was nearly as suspicious of Dissenters resenting their control of the two main towns in Ulster, Derry and Belfast. In 1704 the Dissenters were prevented from holding public offices or sitting on town councils unless they agreed to take the holy sacrament in an Anglican church.

Throughout the 18th century the Anglican ruling class controlled everything that mattered in Ireland — even though they were a small minority of the population. This also guaranteed English control of Ireland.

The Irish were no longer an independent nation. Ireland had become yet another colony in the slowly growing British Empire.

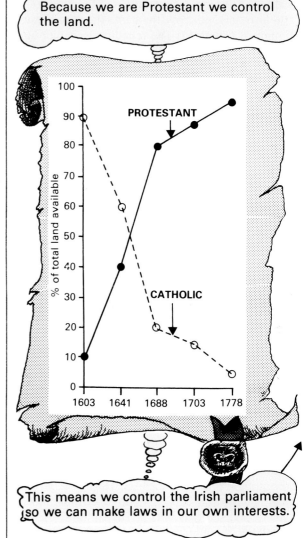

PROTESTANT SETTLER LANDOWNERS GAINED POWER

Because we are Protestant we control the land.

This means we control the Irish parliament so we can make laws in our own interests.

THE TWO SIDES OF VICTORY AT THE BOYNE
1690

NATIVE IRISH CATHOLICS
LOST POWER

The Penal Laws 1697-1727

Whereas it is known that past rebellions have been contrived by Popish clergy
Be it enacted that . . .

1. No Catholic may bequeath his lands as a whole but must divide it amongst his sons
    But if one of these sons becomes Protestant he will inherit the whole estate
    No Catholic can buy land or lease it for more than 31 years

2. No Catholic shall be allowed to vote or become a member of Parliament or a town councillor
    No Catholic shall join the civil service
    No Catholic may be a solicitor or lawyer

3. No Catholic may join the army or the navy
    No Catholic may possess a horse of greater value than £5. Any Protestant offering that sum may take possession of a horse of his Catholic neighbour.
    Catholics keeping guns are liable to a whipping

4. Catholics may not receive higher education or take professional jobs

Because we are Catholics

We have lost ownership of our land. Now we are only tenants

We cannot work peacefully to change these laws

We cannot fight to get our lands back

We cannot improve our position in other ways

WHERE DO WE GO FROM HERE?

3 The fight for independence

The British remained firmly in control of Ireland for 100 years after the Battle of the Boyne. Then, from the 1790s onwards, groups of Irish people began a struggle to free Ireland from British rule. Because they wanted the Irish to become a separate nation once again, they are called *Nationalists*. This struggle against the British is still going on in Ulster and it is the root of today's conflict there.

The fall and rise of the Revolutionary Nationalists 1790-1914

The first people to begin this fight were the Revolutionary Nationalists. They were influenced by the revolutions in America and France at the end of the 18th century. Between 1775-1789 ordinary people in these two countries had overthrown their kings and set up new governments which gave equal rights to everyone. Revolutionary Nationalists decided that Irish people also needed a new system of government which would be:

INDEPENDENT — free from all ties with the British Empire.

DEMOCRATIC — chosen by the majority of the Irish people.

REPUBLICAN — without a king.

They believed that armed revolution was the only way to overthrow British rule in Ireland.

▶ *Can you suggest why they thought this?*

Failed Rebellions

Between 1798-1867 the Revolutionary Nationalists tried three armed rebellions:
— 1798 The rebellion of Wolfe Tone
— 1848 The Young Ireland Revolt
— 1867 The Fenian uprising

All of these had little support from ordinary Irish people and were quickly put down by the British. The Revolutionaries paid a high price for their defeats. After Wolfe Tone's rebellion in 1798, the British decided to abolish the Irish parliament. From 1800 Irish MPs had to sit in the British Parliament. All decisions about Ireland were now made in Westminster.

SOURCE 1 — The aims of Wolfe Tone, 1798

My aim was to break the connection with England and win independence. To do this we had to forget past differences and replace the words 'Protestant' and 'Catholic' with the one name of 'Irishman'.

(adapted from Wolfe Tone's autobiography)

1798 Rebellion of Wolfe Tone and the United Irishmen

1848 'Young Ireland' Rebellion

1867 Fenian uprising organised by the IRB

The early defeats of the Revolutionary Nationalists.

1880-5 Fenians organise a land war against high rents and evictions by landlords. British government agrees to change the Land Laws

SOURCE 2 — The Catholic Church opposes the Revolutionary Nationalists, 1867

Hell is not hot enough nor eternity long enough to punish the Fenians.

(The Bishop of Kerry, 1867)

Look at sources 1 and 2.

▶ *What difference would it have made to Irish history if Wolfe Tone had succeeded?*
▶ *Can you suggest why ordinary Irish people gave so little support to the Revolutionary Nationalists?*

Long live the Fenians

Despite these defeats, the hopes of Revolutionary Nationalists did not die. From 1870, however, they tried different tactics. This was the work of the Fenians or Irish Republican Brotherhood (IRB). The IRB was first set up in the 1850s in America. Its members were Irish people who had been forced to emigrate during the Great Famine of 1845-9. After 1867 they realised there was little support for armed uprisings and instead began to help poor farmers in their fight against harsh landlords. In the 1880s the IRB organised a 'Land League' to stop landlords evicting tenants for not paying their rent. This was successful, forcing the British government to change the land laws. By the early 1900s support for the IRB was slowly growing.

The rise of Sinn Fein

In 1905 the IRB were joined by a new political party called Sinn Fein (meaning 'Ourselves Alone') set up by Arthur Griffith. Like the Fenians, Griffith also wanted Ireland to become an independent republic but he did not plan to achieve this by force. Instead he suggested that the Irish MPs should simply 'opt out' of the British parliament and set up their own government in Dublin. This would collect its own taxes and make its own laws. British rule in Ireland, ignored by the majority of the people, would eventually wither away.

Both Sinn Fein and the IRB were determined to win but in the early 1900s their chances of success looked slim. Like the early Revolutionary Nationalists, they still had little support from most people. Without this popular support for the nationalist cause the British would never be forced to hand over control of Ireland.

The rise of the Parliamentary Nationalists 1820-1914

The Parliamentary Nationalists began their campaign to free Ireland from British rule after the defeat of Wolfe Tone and the abolition of the Irish Parliament in 1800.

Unlike the Revolutionaries, the Parliamentary Nationalists did not demand complete independence from Britain. They were willing to remain within the British Empire as long as the Irish people could have a separate parliament again — though this time it had to represent Catholics as well as Protestants. They believed that peaceful persuasion was the best way to get what they wanted.

While the Revolutionaries faced defeat after defeat, the Parliamentary Nationalists made steady progress during the 19th century.

Daniel O'Connell wins support

The first successes were the work of Daniel O'Connell. Between 1820 and his death in 1847, O'Connell made two important breakthroughs:

1. He won the backing of Catholic bishops and priests. They were the one group of people who had contact with ordinary Catholics throughout Ireland. With their help, O'Connell persuaded thousands of Catholics to support his campaign for a separate Irish Parliament.

2. With thousands of Irish voters supporting him, O'Connell was able to force the British government to change the law banning Catholic MPs. O'Connell's supporters could now go on to build up a party of Irish Nationalist MPs in the British House of Commons. This was important if they were to change the Act of Union which had abolished the old Irish Parliament in 1800.

▶ *Why was the backing of the Catholic church so important to the Parliamentary Nationalists?*

Milestones on the march of the Parliamentary Nationalists

1820s
Catholic Church leaders and ordinary Catholics unite to support the Parliamentary Nationalists

1828
Catholics free to become MPs

1880s
Irish nationalist Party of 85 MPs begin a campaign for a separate Dublin parliament

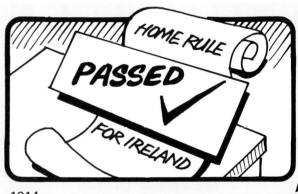

1914
Bill for a Dublin parliament passed

1886
British Liberal Party agree to bring in a Bill for a separate Dublin parliament, but this is defeated

Parnell is ejected from Parliament after disrupting proceedings.

The Irish Nationalist party and the campaign for Home Rule

It took a long time to build up an Irish Nationalist Party. By 1885, however, there were 85 Nationalist MPs in Westminster led by Charles Parnell. They were now a big enough group to make the two British parties, the Liberals and the Conservatives, take notice of their demands.

Parnell made full use of the new-found power of the Irish Nationalist Party. In the 1880s, he joined forces with the Fenians of the Land League who were fighting to protect poor Irish farmers from harsh landlords. Their 'Land War' alarmed British leaders and won sympathy from many ordinary British voters. In Parliament, Parnell demanded changes in the land laws. Between 1881-5 new laws were passed forbidding evictions and high rents and offering tenants loans so they could buy back their land. After this, in 1886, the leaders of the Liberal Party agreed to help Parnell and the Nationalists in their attempt to set up an Irish Parliament. They brought a

'Home Rule for Ireland' Bill before the House of Commons. This was defeated twice — in 1886 and again in 1893. Too many British MPs, including some Liberals, distrusted the Nationalist Party. They feared that Home Rule would be the first step towards complete independence for Ireland. At this time British wealth and power depended on her world-wide trade with her empire. An independent Ireland, hostile to Britain and controlling her sea routes, would be a danger to British power.

John Redmond comes close to victory

Parnell's campaign for an Irish parliament was carried on after 1900 by a new leader, John Redmond. He kept up pressure on Liberal leaders after they returned to government in 1906. At long last, in 1912, the Liberals brought a third Home Rule Bill before the House of Commons. This time, after two years of debate, the bill was passed. By autumn 1914 Irish people were set to have their own parliament again in Dublin. It looked as if, after nearly 100 years, the Parliamentary Nationalists had triumphed.

The rise of Unionist opposition 1790-1914

The hopes of the Irish Nationalist Party were dashed by the fierce opposition of Ulster Protestants.

In the 1790s the first Irish people to demand independence from Britain had been Protestant dissenters — Wolfe Tone and his United Irishmen. Tone had wanted Catholics and Protestants to join together to build a new fairer system of government for all Irish people.

After this rebellion, many Protestants became frightened by the idea of a new Irish government dominated by Catholics. They started to worry that they might lose their lands and power if the Nationalists got their way. Protestants began to see all Nationalists — Parliamentary or Revolutionary — as their enemies. The British — and particularly the British parliament — were now their friends and protectors.

How the split between the Catholics and Protestants grew 1790-1912

1795
Orange Order set up to defend Protestant interests

1798
Wolfe Tone tried to unite Catholics and Protestants in a fight against British rule in Ireland

1912
Unionists set up a private army to fight against a Dublin parliament

1880s
Ulster Unionist Party set up. This began a campaign to keep Britain and Ireland united

The Ulster Unionist Party

The problem was: how could Protestants best defend themselves and their interests? Some Protestants joined the Orange Order. This was a semi-secret society set up in the 1790s. It celebrated William of Orange's victory at the Battle of the Boyne and aimed to keep power in Protestant hands.

SOURCE 1 — The Original oath of the Orange Order, 1795

I solemnly swear that I will support and defend the present King George III and all the heirs of the crown — so long as they support the Protestant ascendancy (hold on power). I do further swear that I am not, nor ever was, a Roman Catholic or Papist; that I was not, nor ever will be a United Irishman and that I never took an oath of secrecy to that Society.

▶ *How does this show Protestant fear of the Nationalists?*

However most people took no definite steps against the Nationalists so long as they seemed unlikely to succeed. In the 1880s all this changed. Parnell and the Irish Nationalist Party had forced the British government to change the land laws. Next it looked as if they would win Home Rule for Ireland. Protestants now decided the time had come to put a stop to all ideas of an independent Irish parliament. So they set up their own political party to fight to keep Britain and Ireland united. They called this 'The Ulster Unionist Party'. By themselves the Ulster Unionists could not have stopped Home Rule. But in 1886 the Conservative Party decided to support them. Lord Randolph Churchill, a leading Conservative, urged Ulster Protestants to take up arms if Home Rule became law. 'Ulster will fight and Ulster will be right' was his slogan.

Edward Carson — why do modern Protestants look back to Carson as their great hero?

Ulster will fight!: a turning point

As things worked out, the Unionists did not have to carry out their threat at first because the Home Rule Bill was defeated in 1886 and again in 1893. By 1912, however, the Nationalists seemed certain to win. So, led by Sir Edward Carson MP, Ulster Protestants organised themselves to fight. Over 400,000 Protestants signed a 'Solemn Covenant' promising to defeat the present conspiracy to set up a Home Rule parliament in Ireland'. They then set up their own private army, the Ulster Volunteers. Within a year they had 100,000 men and £1 million which they used to buy arms from Germany. Carson and the Unionists were given full support by the British Conservative Party. The stand of the Ulster Protestants marked an important turning point in the fight for Irish Independence. Home Rule was no longer a certainty. It all depended on whether the British government was prepared to force Protestants into an independent Ireland against their will.

Ulster Unionist Propaganda — Who do you think this is trying to persuade?

The Irish Revolution 1914-21

By 1914 there were serious problems in Ireland:

- The Parliamentary Nationalists had been promised Home Rule by autumn 1914 but the Unionists were determined to stop Ulster being ruled by an all-Ireland parliament.
- Both sides had strong support: the Nationalist Party amongst Ireland's Catholic voters, the Unionists amongst the Protestants of Ulster.
- Both sides had private armies. The Unionists had recruited 100,000 'Ulster Volunteers' in 1912 to fight against Home Rule. Then, in 1913, the Nationalist Party, with the help of a group of Fenians, formed a rival army to fight for Home Rule. They were called the 'Irish Volunteers'. Within a year 75,000 Catholics had joined and they too were smuggling arms in from Germany.

If the new Home Rule act were to become law it looked as if the British government would have to send in its own army to force the Ulster Unionists to obey the Act and accept an Irish Parliament in Dublin.

Ireland Tug-of-War 1912-14. What do you think the Revolutionary Nationalists were thinking?

Saved by the war?

The British government was saved from civil war in Ireland by the outbreak of World War I. Redmond and the Nationalist Party agreed that the problem of Home Rule could be set on one side till the end of the war. They thought that the war would not last long. Afterwards, with the support of the majority of the Irish people, they would force the British to set up an Irish Parliament. As Redmond declared:

> 'Irish Nationalists can never agree to the mutilation of the Irish nation. Ireland is a unit. The two-nation idea is an abomination.'

Most of the Irish people accepted the delay and over 200,000 Irish men joined the British army to fight for King and Empire.

Irish Volunteers 1914 — what can we learn about the Volunteers from this photograph?

The Easter rising

The Revolutionary Nationalists, as before, rejected Redmond's policy of peaceful persuasion. In 1916, when the war was going badly for Britain, a small group of Fenians organised an armed rising in Dublin on Easter Monday. They took over the General Post Office and proclaimed Ireland an independent Republic. But, as in the past, they got little support from ordinary Catholics who were angry at the damage and shootings. As one eye-witness of the 1916 Easter Rising recalled:

> 'If Ireland as a whole could have got hold of Tom Clarke and his Fenians during that week it would have torn them to pieces.'

Within a few days the rebels had been rounded up by the British army and put in prison. Some were executed. It looked as if Redmond and the Parliamentary Nationalists had been right and the Revolutionary Nationalists, like Sinn Fein, had been wrong.

A recruiting poster from the First World War —
How did the War affect Irish history?

Crowds cheer the British royal family in Dublin 1911 —
Does a Nationalist rising look likely?

The triumph of Sinn Fein 1918

Yet in the end Redmond and his Nationalist Party were proved wrong. In the 1918 General Election the Irish people had a choice of three different futures for Ireland:

1. Home rule, but as part of the British Empire (Redmond and the Nationalist Party).
2. British rule for Ireland (Ulster Unionists).
3. Complete independence (Sinn Fein and the Revolutionary Nationalists).

They voted for Sinn Fein and an Irish Republic by a huge majority — except in Ulster.

This was an important turning point in Irish history. For 100 years the majority of Irish Catholic voters had rejected the Revolutionaries and supported the Parliamentary Nationalists. Now within just four years they had had a dramatic change of heart. The Revolutionary Nationalists had won at last. They lost no time in putting their plans into action. The new Sinn Fein MPs refused to go to London. Instead they declared Ireland an independent Republic and set up their own parliament, the Dail, in Dublin. They also set up a government, police and law courts. Shortly afterwards the Irish volunteers were reorganised and renamed 'The Irish Republican Army' — or IRA.

An IRA Flying Column 1920 —
Do you think the painter supported or opposed the IRA?

1918 Irish election results.

The War of Irish Independence 1919-21

The British had plenty of troops in Ireland and soon sent in more to put down this self-proclaimed government. The Ulster Protestants wanted no part in a separate Ireland so they gave full support to the British. For the next two years there followed a bitter guerrilla war between the British army and the IRA. Both sides fought hard to gain control of a united Ireland.

▶ *How might Irish history have been different if the Parliamentary Nationalists had won in 1918?*

In the end neither got what it wanted. The British government decided that the only solution was to divide Ireland into two parts:

The North In 1920 the six most Protestant counties of Ulster were given their own parliament and their own government. This became known as Stormont after the district of Belfast where it met. Stormont was to have power over most aspects of life in the North but the new state was to stay part of the UK.

The South Irish Nationalists were opposed to the idea of dividing Ireland. But in 1921 a group of leading Sinn Fein and IRA members went to London to talk with the British government. In December 1921 they signed a treaty with the British. The 26 countries of Southern Ireland became known as the Irish Free State. This was an independent country but part of the British Empire.

The partition of Ireland into two separate states was the most important turning point in recent Irish history. For some time the Irish people had been split into two opposing power groups: Protestant Unionists and Catholic Nationalists. Now their country had been split into two parts: North and South. Like these other divisions, the partition line still remains. It is at the heart of today's conflict.

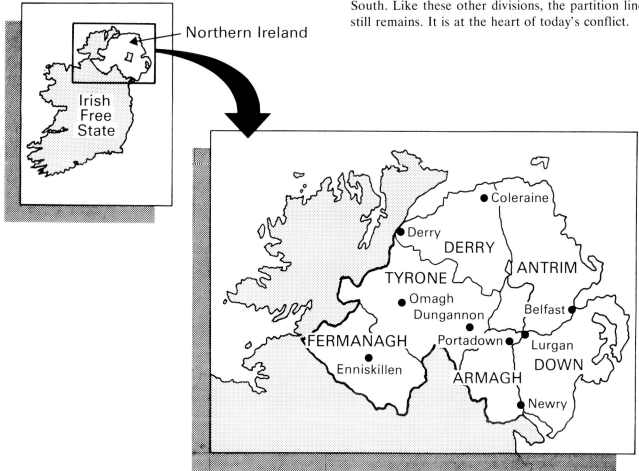

Ireland divided.
Northern Ireland: the six most Protestant counties of the ancient province of Ulster.

4 Ireland divided

When the Partition Treaty was signed in 1921, both British and Sinn Fein leaders saw it as a temporary solution to Ireland's problems. Both hoped that, in time, these problems could be sorted out so that Ireland could become a united country again.

This has not happened. Instead:

● The two parts of Ireland have drifted further apart.
● Since 1968/9 there has been conflict in the North between Unionists who want to keep Ireland divided and Nationalists who want North and South to be reunited.

▶ *How and why did this happen?*
▶ *How did Partition, a temporary solution, turn into a long running problem?*

Drifting apart

After Partition, it was 'hard-line' Unionists who held power in the North. They were the people most determined to keep Ulster British and Protestant. In the South, it was often 'hard-line' Nationalists — those who wanted above all to unite Ireland under their control. Because of this there was little chance that the two parts of Ireland would agree to come together again.

The hardliners —

Basil Brooke: "This country is as determined as in the past to remain part of the UK. Our country is in danger. Today we fight to defend the heritage of our Ulster children. No surrender! We are King's men."

Eamon de Valera: "We shall continue to deny the right of any foreign authority in Ireland. We shall refuse to admit that our country may be carved up by such an authority."

Opponents of the Partition treaty take to the streets — the start of a bitter civil war.

The South — building a separate state

The 1921 Partition treaty caused fierce quarrels amongst Nationalists in the South. The IRA was divided between those who accepted it and those who rejected it. The two sides fought a brutal civil war between 1922-3. This was won by supporters of the treaty. Despite their victory, however, the breach between the two sides has never healed. Since the 1920s there have always been two main political parties in the South.

The Dublin government removed an enormous statue of Queen Victoria in 1949.

Today there are still important differences in their policies. Some IRA leaders continued to insist that the war against the British should go on. Today's IRA men believe their fight is a continuation of the War of Independence 1919-21.

For the first 10 years supporters of the treaty were in power in the South. Then in the 1932 Irish election they were defeated by Fianna Fail and their leader Eamon de Valera.

De Valera became the new Taoiseach (PM) and, with two short breaks, remained in power until 1959. De Valera was born in New York and sent home to Ireland as a child by his mother. He was fiercely opposed to any British control in Ireland. He had been involved in fighting against the British in 1916 and the new Free State government in 1923 and had been put in prison by both as a result. When he came to power in 1932, de Valera was determined to build a strong and independent state in the South.

The chart on the right shows what he did.

How does this stamp symbolise de Valera's plans?

De Valera's Free State	
A united Ireland	In 1937 he introduced a new constitution. This called for a united Ireland and said that Northern Ireland had no right to exist.
A Catholic Ireland	The new constitution also gave a 'special position' to the Catholic Church. Government policy on divorce, the family and education were all in line with Catholic teaching.
A Gaelic Ireland	Great efforts were made to persuade people to speak Gaelic as their main language without success. Ireland remains largely English-speaking.
A free Ireland	De Valera began cutting all remaining economic and political ties with Britain. * Imports were cut but it was not so easy to find other markets for Irish goods. * During World War II Ireland remained neutral. * In 1937 the British King was replaced by an Irish president as head of state. * In 1949 (when de Valera was out of power) the Irish Republic was proclaimed and the country left the British commonwealth.
A peaceful Ireland	De Valera took a tough line on IRA violence. Even though his party had former IRA members, he came to see them as a threat to his own government as well as to the British in Northern Ireland. During World War II his government executed 6 IRA men and allowed 2 more to die on hunger strike.

▶ *Why would these plans make Ulster Protestants more determined to keep the North separate from the South?*

29

Orangemen rule the North

Partition also brought problems for people living in the North. Although Protestant Unionists were in the majority, there were still thousands of Catholic Nationalists living there. Many refused to accept the split. Between July 1920-July 1922 there was fierce street fighting in Belfast and 453 people were killed. This increased Protestant fears about Catholic Nationalists and their links with the South.

Northern Ireland had been given its own parliament. In theory this was meant to look after the interests of the Catholics as well as the Protestants. But since the Protestants were in the majority, they had control of the Stormont Parliament and the government. Before 1969 every member of the Northern Ireland cabinet was a Protestant and almost all were also members of the Orange Order. Unionists also moved local government election boundaries so that they could win control of local councils as well. This was called gerrymandering. The most notorious example of gerrymandering was in Derry. In 1966 10,000 Protestants were able to elect more councillors than 20,000 Catholics.

Protestant Unionists used this power to help their own community. Catholics found it difficult to get jobs and decent council houses. They also felt they were treated unfairly by the police. The Northern Ireland government introduced new laws and a new part-time police force as a defence against the IRA. These police, known as the 'B' Specials, were armed and entirely Protestant. They soon gained a reputation for being anti-Catholic. Although the North was still part of the UK, the British government made no effort to stop this discrimination against the Catholic minority.

A cartoon from a Dublin paper entitled "The Baby-sitter". It shows John Bull and Britannia leaving the baby of Northern Ireland in the hands of the Unionists. What does the cartoonist think about the Unionist babysitter?

What the Unionists thought . . .

PARTITION IS BETTER THAN A UNITED IRELAND. WE WILL TRY TO MAKE NORTHERN IRELAND WORK TO OUR ADVANTAGE . . .

THE CATHOLICS CANNOT BE TRUSTED. THEY ARE TRAITORS TO NORTHERN IRELAND. AS OUR P.M. BASIL BROOKE SAYS "OUR COUNTRY IS IN DANGER. NO SURRENDER! WE ARE KING'S MEN!"

WE MUST KEEP CONTROL OF STORMONT. AS LORD CRAIGAVON PUT IT "WE ARE A PROTESTANT PARLIAMENT FOR A PROTESTANT PEOPLE" 1927

TRAITORS MUST NOT BE ALLOWED TO RUN LOCAL COUNCILS. WE MUST FIX BOUNDARIES SO THAT UNIONISTS ALWAYS WIN.

THE NEW POLICE FORCE NEEDS TO KEEP A CLOSE CHECK ON CATHOLIC TRAITORS.

WE MUST KEEP THE SUPPORT OF LOYAL PROTESTANTS — THEY MUST BE GIVEN GOOD JOBS . . .

. . . AND GOOD HOUSES OF COURSE — IN DIFFERENT PARTS OF TOWN.

Partition: the effects in the North

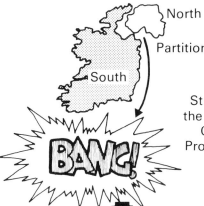

North

Partition 1921

South

Street fighting in the North between Catholics and Protestants 1922-3

Unionists keep control of Stormont parliament

 8 elected Nationalist councillors   Derry 1966    12 elected Unionist councillors

Unionists keep control of local councils by 'fixing' or 'gerrymandering' the election boundaries

WE HAVE SPECIAL POWER TO DO THIS!

Unionists set up 'B' specials — a new armed Protestant police force and pass the Special Powers Act

DOLE   FACTORY

Unionists keep control of jobs for the Protestants

Unionists keep control of council houses and give the best to Protestant

What the Nationalists thought . . .

PARTITION IS WRONG. WE WILL HAVE NOTHING TO DO WITH "NORTHERN IRELAND" WE WILL NOT HAVE ANYTHING TO DO WITH THE NEW GOVERNMENT.

WE WILL NOT JOIN THE NEW CIVIL SERVICE OR POLICE FORCE. WE WILL "OPT OUT" OF LIFE IN THE NORTH JUST LIKE THE SOUTH OPTED OUT OF THE U.K. IN 1919

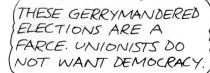
ALIENATION

THESE GERRYMANDERED ELECTIONS ARE A FARCE. UNIONISTS DO NOT WANT DEMOCRACY.

THE PROTESTANT POLICE FORCE IS ALWAYS PICKING ON INNOCENT CATHOLICS.

CATHOLICS ARE UNFAIRLY DISCRIMINATED AGAINST. PROTESTANTS GET ALL THE JOBS — WHILE WE STAY UNEMPLOYED.

WHAT IS THERE FOR US IN A DIVIDED IRELAND?

Partition: the effects in the North

In the early years after Partition Northern Catholics were alienated by Unionist discrimination. They felt there was no place for them in the North and there was no point joining in the government of the province. Unemployment was high and Catholics were much more likely to be out of a job than Protestants. Thousands of Catholics left Ulster and went to the South.

Hopes of peaceful change 1950-68

By the 1950s, however, the mood of many Catholics had changed. Instead of hoping for a united Ireland, they accepted that they were part of a separate Northern state. They began to hope that their lives could be improved by peaceful, political changes.

This new attitude became clear between 1956-62 when the IRA started a campaign of violence in the North. It failed mainly because ordinary Catholics were not willing to support the IRA and violence. Many IRA leaders were imprisoned. After this the IRA abandoned the idea of force as the best way to reunite Ireland. Instead they tried to lessen the gap between Nationalists and Unionists by campaigning for improvements in the wages and living conditions of all working people.

By the early 1960s there were also changes in the attitudes of political leaders in the North and South. This began in 1959 when de Valera retired as Taoiseach (PM) of the Irish Republic. Sean Lemass, the new leader, was less hostile to the Unionists in the North. Then in 1963 the hard line Unionist PM, Brookeborough, was replaced by Terence O'Neill. O'Neill was keen to end unfair treatment of Catholics in Northern Ireland. The new hopeful mood was shown to the world in 1965 when Lemass paid a visit to O'Neill at Stormont. It now seemed possible that Catholics and Protestants could together make a new and fairer way of life in the North.

It was at this time, when real improvements at last seemed possible, that violence again broke out in Northern Ireland.

1963-67
New Unionist government promises Catholics fairer treatment

1967-8
Catholics get impatient at the slow pace of reform. Civil Rights movement starts

Oct 1968 - July 1969
Fighting breaks out between Catholics and Protestants on Civil Rights marches

Countdown to the troubles

Aug 1969
British troops sent in to keep the peace

1969
Unionist government brings in changes to the police, housing, elections and jobs

Nov 1969
IRA provos start their fight against the British and the Unionists

Aug 1970
Ordinary Catholics oppose violence and form new political party the SDLP

Aug 1971
Internment — Unionist government starts to imprison suspected terrorists without trial

Sept 1971
Protestant private armies set up the UDA and UDF

Jan 1972
Bloody Sunday — British troops shoot at Civil Rights marchers

March 1972
British government scraps the N. Ireland parliament and begins to rule the North directly from London

The North explodes 1968-72

Catholics fight with the police August 1969.

The Northern Catholics had welcomed O'Neill's ideas but his reforms were too slow in coming. So in 1967 a group of young Catholics got together and set up a Civil Rights Association. Beginning in October 1968, they organised a series of protest marches to demand equal rights for Catholics. These marches were meant to be peaceful but they ended in violence and bloodshed between Catholics and Protestants.

British troops arrive 1969: Why had law and order broken down so badly?

O'Neill found it impossible to stop violence spreading and resigned in April 1969. By August 1969 fighting between Catholics and Protestant police was out of control so the British government stepped in and sent British troops to restore order. British troops were meant to be a short-term emergency measure but they have been there ever since.

The British government also persuaded the Unionist leaders to introduce reforms. These concentrated on four things:

1. **The police**
   The part-time B specials were abolished
   RUC was brought under army control.
2. **Housing**
   A fairer system of allocating council houses was set up.
3. **Elections**
   Gerrymandering was stopped.
4. **Unemployment**
   British government grants to set up new industries.

These reforms failed to stop the fighting.

In August 1971, as a last resort, the Stormont government brought in new rules allowing suspected 'terrorists' to be imprisoned without trial. They were kept in internment camps like enemy prisoners in wartime. Internment also failed to stop the fighting.

▶ *How can we tell this from the graph below?*

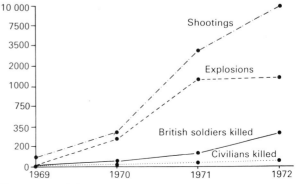

The pattern of violence in the 1970s.

By 1970 the Provisional IRA had begun its campaign of violence.

Return of the IRA and UVF

By early 1972 the situation had reached crisis point. There was no longer just the problem of riots involving ordinary Catholics and Protestants. Private armies had appeared on the streets of Belfast and Derry. After their failure in 1956-62, the IRA were back and now controlled the Catholic areas of these cities. This time they were a new group of young IRA men calling themselves 'The Provisionals' (after the provisional government set up in Dublin during the 1916 Easter Rising). In 1969-70 the Provisionals had split away from the old 'Official' IRA because they disagreed with the policies of its leaders. After this the 'Officials' stayed in the South trying to reunite Ireland by peaceful persuasion of the Catholic and Protestant working classes. The 'Provos' took control of operations in the North, convinced that only force would bring an end to the British occupation of their country. Meanwhile, at the other side of the barricades, were the Protestant paramilitaries, the Ulster Volunteer Force and the Ulster Defence Association. They were determined to fight to keep Ulster British.

Direct rule 1972

Many people on both sides did not support these private armies. In 1970 a group of Catholic Nationalists set up the Social Democratic Labour Party (SDLP) to campaign for peaceful change. But they were not strong enough to stop the violence. It was now clear that the Stormont government had lost all control of the Province. With Ulster on the brink of civil war, the British government decided there was only one thing to do. It suspended the Northern Ireland government and parliament and began to rule Ulster direct from Britain.

The years 1968-72 had brought two more turning points in the history of today's conflict:

- in 1968 hopes of peace between Nationalists and Unionists had been dashed by the outbreak of fighting
- in 1972 the Unionist controlled government of Ulster, set up in 1921, was suspended.

Direct rule by the British government has continued ever since — and so has the fighting.

Britain and Ireland since 1972

Since 1972 the British government has been faced with the task of keeping order in a province with two communities who dislike and fear each other. Four main solutions have been tried.

1. Power sharing. In 1974 the British tried to set up a new system of government in which power would be shared between Protestants and Catholics. The leader was Brian Faulkner, leader of the Unionist Party, and his deputy was Gerry Fitt, the leader of the Nationalist SDLP. This 'Power Sharing' failed after only five months because the Protestants opposed it.

In 1982 the British set up a new Northern Ireland Assembly elected by fair voting. At first this was to have powers of discussion only. But if the Protestants and Catholics could agree to work together on any problem they were to be given power to deal with it. This also failed. Catholics refused even to attend the Assembly.

▶ *The failure of these 'Power sharing' experiments could be seen as another turning point on the road to today's conflict. What difference would it have made if they had worked?*

Power-sharing.

2. Changes in the police and security forces. When British troops were first sent to Ulster in 1969 they were given complete control of all peace-keeping operations and the Royal Ulster Constabulary. Since then the British government has gradually reduced the number of regular soldiers. In 1977 they handed back control to the RUC. Although the RUC is meant to be a 'mixed' police force only 10% of its members are Catholic. Today the RUC is supported by the Ulster Defence Regiment. This was formed from local recruits in 1970 after the notorious Protestant B Specials were disbanded. The UDR is also meant to be a mixed regiment but today 97% of the soldiers are Protestants.

The graph shows how the relative strength of the security forces has changed since 1970.

▶ *How do you think Catholics have reacted to these changes?*
▶ *Do you think these changes have helped to reduce tension between Catholics and Protestants?*

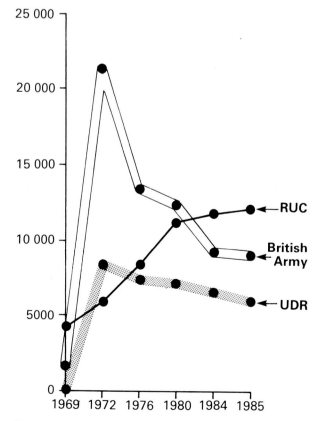

Changes in the security forces.

3. Rough justice. As well as trying 'Power Sharing' experiments, the British leaders have also tried to stop the bombings and shootings. To do this they have used tough methods:

● plastic bullets in riots
● trials without juries
● unsupported evidence of informers to convict 'terrorist' suspects.

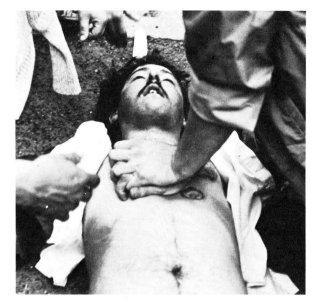

Rough justice: The victim of a plastic bullet.

4. Talks with the South. Since 1980 the British government has also been involved in talks with leaders of the Irish Republic. Leaders in the South believe that the conflict in Ulster cannot be solved unless they are part of any peace plan. In 1984 they suggested that the only long term solution was to unite North and South in a single state. This idea was flatly rejected by British Prime Minister, Margaret Thatcher.

In 1985, however, the British signed 'the Anglo-Irish Agreement' with the Republic. This set up a joint committee of the two governments to discuss such matters as the security forces, justice and the law in Ulster. They hope to find ways of persuading Unionists and Nationalists to respect each others rights and views. However, Unionists claim that for the first time since Partition in 1921, the British have allowed the Government of the Republic to have a say in the running of the North.

Some people have suggested that the Anglo-Irish agreement will prove to be another turning point in the history of the present conflict.

▶ *What effect has it had so far?*
▶ *Has it made things better or worse?*
▶ *Look at the graph of violent deaths. Have British tactics worked?*

Talks with Dublin: Dr Fitzgerald and Margaret Thatcher.

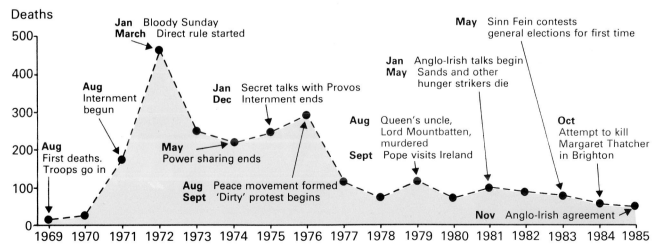

Violent deaths and British policy in Northern Ireland 1969-1985.

The Nationalist reaction (1972 onwards)

The activities of Unionist extremists and the tough policy of the British made the Nationalists more bitter than ever. Many Catholics once again felt that there could be no place for them in an Ulster controlled by the Unionists or the British. They now longed for a united Ireland. But just as in the past there were disagreements about the right methods to use.

The Parliamentary Nationalists

The SDLP, led by John Hume, are today's (1987) Parliamentary Nationalists. Like Parnell before them, they want to solve Ireland's problems by peaceful negotiation.

They support the Anglo-Irish agreement because the Southern Irish committee members will be able to speak up on behalf of Northern Nationalists. The SDLP have won friends in Britain but not amongst the IRA.

SOURCE 1 — The IRA do not support the SDLP

Last week John Hume's election headquarters were burned down. A day earlier an IRA statement described him as 'part of the British war Machine'.

(extract from 'Sunday Times', May 6th 1984)

The Nationalist debate since 1970: How do we get a united Ireland?

By peaceful talks?

By prison protests?

SOURCE 2 — Belfast graffiti gives a different view of the meaning of the letters S.D.L.P.

A critical view of the SDLP — Who do you think would paint graffiti like this?

By the bomb?

By "the ballot as well as the bullet"?
(Gerry Adams, MP)

The Revolutionary Nationalists — The Provisional IRA

The Provisionals are today's main Revolutionary Nationalists. In the early 1970s they planted bombs in Ulster and on the British mainland which killed and injured ordinary passers-by. This lost them support among ordinary Catholics in the North. So after 1976 they changed their tactics and concentrated on the police and the army. Lord Mountbatten, the Queen's uncle was murdered in 1979. In 1984 a bomb planted in a Brighton hotel which the Conservative Party were using as their annual conference headquarters nearly killed Margaret Thatcher and other members of the British Government.

SOURCE 3 — The Provisionals claim responsibility for the Brighton bombing, October 1984

Thatcher will now realise that Britain cannot occupy our country, torture our prisoners and get away with it. Today we were unlucky. But remember we have only to be lucky once — you have to be lucky always. Give Ireland peace and there will be no war!

(Irish Republican Press Bureau)

The Provos saw that they depended on the support of ordinary Catholics both in Ireland and America, so they paid great attention to publicity. Between 1976 and 1981 imprisoned IRA men demanded special treatment as political prisoners and refused to wear prison clothes. The British refused to let them have their own clothes, so they wore none at all. They also began a 'dirty protest' — smearing their cells with their own excrement. Then in 1981 a group of IRA prisoners, led by Bobby Sands, went on hunger strike. Ten of them died.

Sinn Fein

In the 1980s some of the younger IRA men, led by Gerry Adams, have brought forward a new idea. Using the old name Sinn Fein, they have built up a new political party for Revolutionary Nationalists in Ulster. Adams argues that it is important to have MPs and local councillors who support the aims of the IRA. This would show the people of Britain and America that ordinary Catholics support the IRA and that it is not just a 'criminal conspiracy controlled by a group of godfathers'.

In the election of 1983 Adams was elected as British MP for West Belfast, and in 1985 Sinn Fein did well in local council elections in N. Ireland. Gerry Adams talks of 'using the ballot as well as the bullet'. He wants Sinn Fein to become the main nationalist party in the North instead of the SDLP. Unlike the SDLP, Gerry Adams has rejected the Anglo-Irish Agreement.

SOURCE 4 — A useless deal

This deal does not go anywhere near bringing peace to this part of Ireland. On the contrary it reinforces partition because Dublin is recognising Northern Ireland (as a separate state).

(Gerry Adams, 16th November 1985)

▶ How do Adams' views of the Anglo-Irish agreement differ from those of the Unionists?
▶ Why do you think the Provisionals are so fiercely opposed to the SDLP?

The Unionists' reaction 1972 onwards

Some Unionists believed that the coming of violence and the revival of the IRA since 1969 was due partly to the softness of their own leaders. So they set up a rival party, the Democratic Unionist Party, led by Ian Paisley. He became well-known for his fiercely anti-Catholic, anti-Nationalist and anti-British government views.

SOURCE 1 — Paisley speaks for the Protestants

If we cannot arrest the IRA and disarm them they are going to kill us. We have not the right but the duty to kill them before they kill me, my family and others.

The ordinary Ulster man is not going to surrender to the IRA or be betrayed into a united Ireland or put his neck under the jackboot of Popery.

(Ian Paisley, January 1982)

Other extreme Unionists set up Protestant private armies, the Ulster Defence Association (UDA) and the Ulster Volunteer Force (UVF). Since 1974 the UDA has been led by Andy Tyrie. He has called for an independent Ulster and has great support in working class areas of Belfast.

No surrender.

No power sharing

Since 1972, extreme Unionists, like Ian Paisley, have opposed all moves to involve Nationalists in the government of Ulster.

In 1974 they wrecked the 'Power Sharing' system by means of a general strike of all Protestant workers. It lasted a fortnight and brought ordinary life in the province to a halt.

Since the 1985 local elections, extreme Unionists have tried different ways to keep new Sinn Fein councillors out of office. Paisley's Democratic Unionists have refused to work with them and tried to get them banned. Loyalist gunmen have threatened to 'take them out'.

Smash Sinn Fein.

Rule Britannia.

Ulster says "No" to a deal with Dublin.

No links with the South

Unionists have also been worried by the talks between the British government and leaders of the Irish Republic.

SOURCE 2 — Fears of a dirty deal

The only thing that Protestants are afraid of is a dirty, underhanded deal done behind our backs. We are in the hands of our English masters. And we understand that they are not our friends. They would like to destroy us. Protestants love their liberty too much to put themselves into a state where there is censorship but no divorce.

(adapted from a speech by Ian Paisley, December 1981)

To Unionists, the 1985 Anglo-Irish agreement was just such a dirty deal. The UDA threatened to murder all the civil servants involved. Unionist MPs resigned their seats in protest. After re-election they did not return to the British parliament.

▶ *Which group of MPs first had the idea of 'opting out' of the British parliament?*

SOURCE 3 — We are prepared to lay down our lives

The hearts of Ulster have been stricken with the deepest of sorrows. Mrs. Thatcher tells us that the Republic has got a say in this province. We say never, never, never, never. We are prepared to lay down our lives for Ulster. I never thought I would live to see the day when 1912 was repeated.

(Ian Paisley, speaking at a Unionist rally in Belfast, 24 November 1985)

▶ *Why did Paisley mention 1912?*
▶ *What action have Unionists taken about the Anglo-Irish agreement since 1986?*

Paisley's deputy in the DUP, Peter Robinson, played a major role in the campaign against the Anglo-Irish agreement. He acted even tougher than Paisley and was tipped by many people as a future hard-line, leader of the Ulster Protestants.

Connections

Television and newspapers are very good at telling us **what** is happening in the world. They are not always so good at telling us **why** things happen. If a large bomb goes off in Brighton, Belfast or Beirut we soon know all about the casualties and can see the destruction. We are not usually told all the circumstances which led someone to plant such a bomb. Unless we know more about these circumstances, it is all too easy to 'write off' the people who did it as 'mad' or 'very bad'. Most people are neither so there must be some other reasons for such actions.

▶ *Can you think of any reasons why TV news often describes events without explaining them fully?*

▶ *Some newspapers suggest that members of the IRA are crazy. Historians disagree. Does this mean that historians support the IRA?*

The following pages go behind the news stories about Ireland to find out why there is a conflict and why people behave as they do.

If you want to work out the causes of a modern world problem you have to begin by asking two key questions:

Was there one cause or many?

▶ *Is the conflict in Ireland about:*

	Religion	*the different religious beliefs of Catholics and Protestants?*
or	**Power Politics**	*the political demands of Unionists and Nationalists?*
or	**Economics**	*the gap between 'the haves' and the 'have nots'?*
or	**Social Life**	*the different way people live and are educated?*

▶ *Or is it about all of these?*
▶ *If so, is there any* **connection** *between them?*

Are the causes long term or short term or both?

▶ *Did the conflict in Ireland begin with the street fighting in the North in 1968-9?*
▶ *Or are the causes of the 1968 fighting* **connected** *to other events earlier in Irish history?*

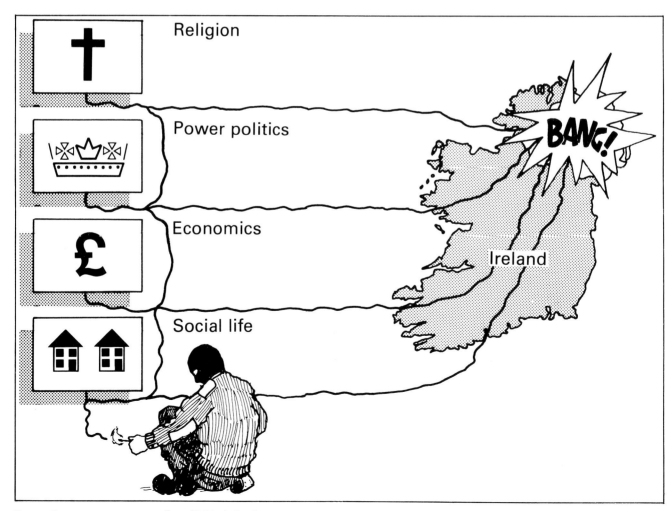

Connections — some causes of conflict in Ireland.

Religion

Today the people of Northern Ireland are divided by many things. One of these is religion. The split between Catholics and Protestants goes back a long way to the 16th and 17th centuries. It was then that British rulers first brought the Protestant church and Protestant settlers to Ireland — a Catholic country.

In Ireland Catholics and Protestants have been in conflict — on and off — for over 300 years.

What exactly are they fighting about?
▶ *Is it simply a quarrel about religious beliefs?*
▶ *Or is there a connection between religion and other causes of the conflict in Ireland?*

Is the conflict mainly about different religious beliefs?

Today some people might say that the conflict is one of religion. Most people would say that the problem is more complicated than this. Today's conflict is really about the political beliefs and political power and these have become linked with religion.

SOURCE 1 — Two groups divided by the Bible

(an English cartoonist's view, 'The Guardian', 1969)

Englyſh Proteſtantes ſtriped naked & turned into the mountaines in the froſt, & ſnowe, whereof many hundreds are periſhed to death, & many lyinge dead in diches & Sauages upbraided them ſainge, now are ye wilde Iriſh as well as wee.

Catholics attack Protestants 1641. Look carefully at this picture: which side do you think the artist is on?

SOURCE 2 — Protestants object to 'The Sound of Music'

We wish to protest about the staging of 'The Sound of Music' in Kilkeel High School. 'The Sound of Music' is full of Romanish influences which Protestants hate. At one point candles are lit on stage, some of the children have to appear in the garb of Catholic nuns and they also have to bless themselves publicly in the way the Romans do.

(George McConnell, Publicity Officer for the Democratic Unionist Party, 'The Times', 17 December 1977)

SOURCE 3 — Why do the IRA kill Protestants?

People say our campaign in Northern Ireland is sectarian (against people with different religious beliefs), I deny that. Protestants are shot because they're Unionists and active agents of British imperialism.

(adapted from a statement by Sean MacStiofain, Provisional IRA Chief of Staff, 1972)

The Protestant private armies have similar political motives. They kill Catholics because they are Nationalists and fear that all Nationalists want a united Ireland.

Look at the materials on this page and think about these questions:
▶ *When and why did people's political views become linked to their religion?*
▶ *How have these worked together to cause conflict in Ireland?*

The connection between politics and religion

1. England 1531: The King breaks with Rome

Henry VIII broke all links between the English Catholic Church and the Pope by declaring himself its 'Supreme Head'.

▶ *Henry had important political reasons for doing this. What were they?*

2. England 1570: The Pope strikes back

Pope Pius V issued a papal decree:

SOURCE 1 — Elizabeth I is excommunicated

We do declare Elizabeth to be cut off from the Holy Catholic Church, and we declare her to be deprived of her pretended title to the kingdom. We command all noblemen and subjects not to obey her or her orders and laws.

▶ *This decree had important political effects for Elizabeth I. What were they?*

3. England 1570-1603: Catholic rebellions

By 1570 most of Elizabeth's subjects were Protestants so the Papal Bull meant nothing to them. But some were still Catholic. The Bull put them in an impossible position. They had to choose between their Queen and their faith. At a time when religion was important to people, this was a difficult choice to make. Some chose their faith.

For the next 30 years Elizabeth faced a series of plots and rebellions in England and Ireland. These aimed to get rid of Elizabeth and put a Catholic ruler in her place — first Mary Queen of Scots, later Philip of Spain. In 1588 Philip sent the Spanish Armada to conquer England. In the end Elizabeth won and managed to gain control over Catholics in England.

4. Ireland 1608-10: The Protestant Plantations begin

But Ireland was still a problem. Most Irish landowners refused to become Protestants. Some were still ready to plot with Spain to get rid of James I — Elizabeth's successor. So James decided to make sure that Irish leaders would in future be loyal subjects of England's Protestant King. He sent loyal Protestant settlers to live in Ireland.

5. Ireland 1641: Catholic rebellions

The Catholics of Ulster felt angry and cheated by the loss of their land and power. In 1641 they took part in a great rebellion against the Protestant settlers. Their grievances were political and economic.

▶ *How did religion become involved?*

SOURCE 2 — A Protestant's eye-view of the Catholic Rebellion, 1641 (Look at the picture on the right)

The writing reads 'The Priests and Jesuits anoint the rebels with their sacrament of unction before they go to murder and rob — assuring them that for their meritorious service if they be killed he shall escape purgatory and go to heaven immediately.'

6. The fight for Irish Independence 1790-1918

In the 1790s Irish Nationalists began a long fight to free Ireland from British rule. The first Revolutionary Nationalists wanted to keep religion out of this political battle.

SOURCE 3 — Irishmen should unite, 1798

The people are divided and distrustful of each other. This Society of United Irishmen wishes to create a brotherhood of affection between Irishmen of both religions — Catholics and Protestants

(Wolfe Tone, Revolutionary Nationalist, 1798)

This was not easy. Catholic Church leaders fiercely opposed the rebellions against British rule.

Then in the 1820s the Parliamentary Nationalists persuaded Catholic Church leaders to help in their campaign for Catholic MPs and an Irish Parliament.

▶ *Why was the support of the Church important to the Nationalists?*

7. Unionists fight to keep Ireland British 1880-1914

By the 1880s Protestants feared that Nationalists would win a separate Irish Parliament. A Dublin Parliament, controlled by a Catholic majority, would threaten their hold on power as well as their Protestant way of life. So they set up their own political party to fight against the Nationalists.

▶ *Why did Protestants still fear the Catholic church? (Look at the cartoon.)*

SOURCE 4 — The power of the priests in Ireland: a Victorian Protestant view

8. North and South 1920-86

Since 1920 Ireland has been divided into two parts; the South, controlled by Catholic Nationalists and the North which has a majority of Protestant Unionists. The old mixture of religious and political fears has continued to cause conflict.

Look at sources 5, 6 and 7.
▶ *Have the fears of the Protestant majority been about religion or political power?*

SOURCE 5 — The influence of the Catholic Church on daily life in the South, 1908-86

1908 Papal decree against mixed marriages between Catholics and Protestants. Children of such marriages had to be brought up as Catholics.

1925 Divorce banned in the new Southern state.

1929 Censorship Board established to ban 'obscene' books and those recommending contraception.

1937 New constitution recognises 'special position' of Catholic Church (withdrawn in 1972 as a concession to Protestants).

1951 Bishops stop new health care system for mothers and babies.

1979 Contraceptives legalised, but only for married couples with a doctor's prescription.

1983 Anti-abortion clause written into the constitution, after a referendum.

1986 Referendum on divorce rejects any change in the law. Divorce is still not allowed in the South.

SOURCE 6 — Why do Northern Protestants fear a united Ireland?

We must recognise the genuine fears of the Northern Protestant that in a united Ireland he would be in a minority and that he would suffer in much the same way as the Catholic minority in Ulster. There is the position of the Catholic Church. There are the Catholic rules on mixed marriages, the right to contraception and family planning, the right to divorce. There is the question of social services. In the North they have better health services, unemployment benefits and old age pensions.

(adapted from a speech by Noel Browne, Irish Labour Party, 1971)

SOURCE 7 — The Roman Catholic church is the anti-Christ

You see the Roman Catholic Church is the anti-Christ. There isn't really a political solution, because its a religious battle against the rising of the anti-Christ.

(Mrs Hamilton, a Presbyterian Dissenter and supporter of Ian Paisley, speaking in 'Only rivers run free', 1984)

Power politics

Nationalists want power so
that they can make Ireland —

1. United

2. Independent

Unionists want power so
that they can keep Ulster —

1. Separate

2. Linked to Britain

Today's conflict is a struggle for power between two groups of people in Ulster. This struggle is only partly about the religious differences between Catholics and Protestants. It is also a conflict about political beliefs between Nationalists and Unionists.

Most countries have groups with different political ideas about how they want to run the country. In Britain today Conservatives, Socialists, Liberals, Social Democrats and others compete to control the government. They object strongly to each others' ideas but they do not resort to shooting and bombing to defeat their opponents.

▶ *Why have political differences led to violence in Ulster?*

To understand this we have to look at the aims and methods of both sides.

Martin McGuinness

Nationalist rebels

Nationalists agree that they want a united Ireland but they disagree about the best way to get this.

Some, like the SDLP, think the only way is by peaceful negotiation. This view has a long history.

▶ *Look at the chart on pp. 48-49. Who first started the idea of Parliamentary Nationalism?*

▶ *If all Nationalists thought this way, how might the situation in Ulster today be different?*

Others, like the Provisional IRA, have a different view:

SOURCE 1 — The cutting edge of the IRA

We believe the only way the Irish people can bring about the freedom of their country is through the use of arms. We Republicans don't believe that just winning elections will bring freedom. It will be the cutting edge of the IRA that will bring freedom.

(Martin McGuinness, IRA leader, speaking on 'Real Lives', October 1985)

As you can see from the chart, the idea of violence as the only way to get a united Ireland also has a long history. Revolutionary Nationalists still talk of 'the age old struggle against British aggression.' They keep on remembering old martyrs and reliving old grievances.

▶ *Why do you think they keep on recalling their past in this way?*

▶ *In the past, why did they believe that armed struggle was the only way to get what they wanted?*

▶ *How can the use of violence be counter productive?*

▶ *How do you think Nationalist memories of the past have helped to cause conflict in Ulster today?*

Irish Nationalism: The two traditions

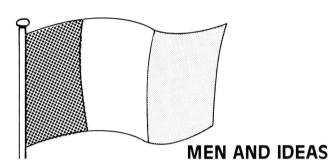

MEN AND IDEAS

MEN AND ACTIONS

Tone's 'address to the people of Ireland'. SIX HUNDRED YEARS OF SLAVERY HAVE PASSED OVER OUR FATHERS' HEADS. IT IS ENGLAND WHO DEPRIVES OUR WRETCHED PEASANTRY OF THEIR RIGHTS AS HUMAN BEINGS. YOU MUST CHOOSE BETWEEN SLAVERY OR INDEPENDENCE. I DO NOT DOUBT YOUR DECISION: LIBERTY FOR YOURSELVES AND INDEPENDENCE FOR YOUR COUNTRY.

Fenian Oath sworn in Dublin 1858. I SWEAR TO RENOUNCE ALL ALLEGIANCE TO THE QUEEN OF ENGLAND AND TO TAKE UP ARMS AND FIGHT TO MAKE IRELAND AN INDEPENDENT DEMOCRATIC REPUBLIC.

Patrick Pearce. Easter rebel and IRB leader. WE COME HERE TO COMPLETE THE WORK OF TONE. TONE HAS STATED OUR PROGRAMME FOR US 'TO BREAK THE CONNECTION WITH ENGLAND THE NEVER FAILING SOURCE OF ALL OUR EVILS! IRELAND WILL NOT FIND CHRIST'S PEACE TILL SHE HAS TAKEN CHRIST'S SWORD. WE MUST NOT FAINT AT THE SIGHT OF BLOOD.

The Easter Rebels' Proclamation of the Irish Republic, Easter 1916. WE DECLARE THE RIGHT OF THE PEOPLE OF IRELAND TO THE OWNERSHIP OF IRELAND. IN EVERY GENERATION THE IRISH HAVE DECLARED THEIR RIGHT TO NATIONAL FREEDOM..SIX TIMES IN THE PAST 300 YEARS THEY HAVE ASSERTED IT IN ARMS.

IRA Manifesto 1956. THIS IS THE AGE-OLD STRUGGLE AGAINST BRITISH AGGRESSION. IT IS UP TO THIS GENERATION OF IRISH MEN AND WOMEN TO RECEIVE FOR ALL TIME OUR UNITY, INDEPENDENCE AND FREEDOM FROM FOREIGN DOMINATION.

Provisional IRA statement 1979. THE BRITISH GOVERNMENT CONTINUE TO OPPRESS OUR PEOPLE. WELL FOR THIS WE WILL TEAR OUT THEIR IMPERIALIST HEART.

Danny Morrison Sinn Fein Conference 1983 IS THERE ANY ONE HERE WHO OBJECTS TO TAKING POWER WITH A BALLOT PAPER IN ONE HAND AND AN ARMALITE RIFLE IN THE OTHER?

IRISH NATIONALISM: THE TWO TRADITIONS

REVOLUTIONARY NATIONALISTS

They fight against this using the bomb and bullet

ENGLISH CONQUEST

PARLIAMENTARY NATIONALISTS

They campaign against this using the ballot box

BALLOT BOX

MEN AND ACTIONS

1790

1800

1798 WOLFE TONE leads his UNITED IRISHMEN in an armed PROTESTANT revolt to free Ireland from English rule

UNION OF ENGLAND AND IRELAND! Irish Parliament abolished

1820-47 DANIEL O'CONNELL first involves ordinary CATHOLICS and the CATHOLIC CHURCH in Irish Nationalism. He organises campaigns against the ban on Catholics becoming MPs and in favour of a separate parliament for Ireland

1848 YOUNG IRELANDERS revive TONE's ideas of uniting 'Protestant, Catholic and Dissenter under the common name of Irishman' and rise in rebellion

1850

1867 The IRISH REPUBLICAN BROTHERHOOD (IRB or Fenians) organises an armed rebellion of Irish CATHOLICS

1879-90 CHARLES STEWART PARNELL and the IRISH PARTY campaign in Westminster for 'Home Rule' for Ireland. Parnell was a PROTESTANT

1913 IRB set up the 'IRISH VOLUNTEERS' a private army of CATHOLIC NATIONALISTS

1900-18 JOHN REDMOND and the IRISH PARTY continue the campaign in Westminster for an independent parliament for Ireland

1900

1916 IRB organise the 'Easter Rising' an armed rebellion in Dublin

1919-21 IRB's Irish Volunteers become the IRISH REPUBLICAN ARMY (IRA) fighting in the Irish War of Independence

1967 NORTHERN IRELAND CIVIL RIGHTS ASSOCIATION begins peaceful protests against discrimination against Catholics

1956 IRA organise a bombing campaign in the North

1950

1969 PROVISIONAL IRA break away from the official IRA and begin a bombing campaign

1970 SDLP (Social Democratic and Labour Party formed to press for peaceful change leading to a united Ireland

1985 THE IRA-SINN FEIN ALLIANCE In 1985 the IRA decided for the first time to put up candidates for election to parliament and local councils using Sinn Fein their political party. Sinn Fein is controlled by the army council.

Loyal Unionists

Unionists are determined to stop North and South being united, but they disagree about the best way to do this.

Some, like the politicians of the Official Unionist Party, think that peaceful negotiation is the best way.

▶ *If all Unionists thought this way how might the situation in Ulster be different today?*

Some, like the UDA and the UVF, think that fighting is the only way to stop the Nationalists.

Others, like Ian Paisley and his Democratic Unionist Party are prepared to do both.

SOURCE 1 — Kill or be killed

You either be killed by the IRA or kill them and I want to see them dead. Something has to be done to finish this trouble once and for all and the only way to do this with the IRA is to kill them.

(Gregory Campbell, a member of the UDA and a Democratic Unionist Party Councillor, speaking on 'Real Lives' October, 1985)

The idea of fighting and talking has a long history amongst Unionists. Like the IRA, they keep looking back to the past — remembering old victories and old heroes.

The UDA on the march — why do you think the British government fear that Protestants may abandon the OUP and turn to private armies like the UDA?

Remember 1690

Since their arrival in Ireland in the 17th century, Protestants have felt threatened by the greater number of Irish Catholics. Many modern Protestants still have a defensive and suspicious attitude to Catholics. This attitude is seen in the activities of the Orange Order.

Today 100,000 Protestants are members of the Orange Order. Most Unionist politicians over the last 100 years have also been Orangemen. Their hero is William of Orange. They believe that his victory at the Battle of the Boyne saved Protestants from destruction at the hands of their Catholic enemies. For many of them the 17th century struggle still goes on today and they relive it in different ways.

SOURCE 2 — Drawing of King Billy

A drawing of King William of Orange from a purse of an Orangeman c.1800. On it are the words "The immortal memory of 1690".

SOURCE 3 — An Orange Order toast, early 1800s

To the glorious memory of King William III, who saved us from slaves and slavery. Knaves and Knavery, Popes and popery. Whoever denies this toast may be crammed and jammed into the muzzle of the great gun of Athlone and fired into the Pope's belly, and the Pope into the Devil's belly and the Devil into hell, and the door locked and the key in an Orangeman's pocket.

SOURCE 4 — Modern Protestant fighting song

If guns are made for shooting,
Then skulls are made to crack.
You've never seen a better Taig (Catholic)
Than with a bullet in his back . . .

SOURCE 5 — Protestant wall painting from the 1970s

A modern Protestant wall painting — What are people being told to remember?

SOURCE 6 — Junior Orangeman's Catechism 1966

Question:
How can I help to keep Ulster Protestant, loyal and British?

Answer:
a. by being a faithful member of my own church.
b. by being a regular member of my own Junior Loyal Orange Lodge.
c. by showing in my own character that the Ulster-British way of life is worth having and holding.

▶ *How do you think Orangemen and their memories of the past have helped to cause conflict in Ulster today?*

Remember 1912

The idea of fighting Unionists goes back to early days of the Unionist Party in the 1880s. This was the time when Parnell was campaigning for Home Rule. Protestants wanted to stop all plans for an all-Ireland Parliament based in Dublin and dominated by Catholics. So they formed the Ulster Unionist Party. Although this was a political party of Protestant MPs, they made it clear that if pushed too far 'Ulster will fight'. This has been the rallying cry of Unionist politicians and private armies ever since.

In 1912 it seemed certain that a Dublin Parliament could finally be set up. So Unionists made plans to stop this by force. Led by Edward Carson, they prepared a separate government for an independent Ulster. At the same time they formed their own private army, the Ulster Volunteer Force to defend themselves. Carson has become the hero of Unionist politicians and private armies today.

Carson's action convinced the British that Ulster would have to be left out of an independent Ireland. From 1921-72 the North was ruled by a Unionist government. In these years Unionists saw the North as **their** country and were determined to keep it that way. Again they were prepared to use force. Catholics were seen as potential traitors and an armed Protestant police force made sure they did not get out of hand.

In the 1960s Unionist politicians began to take a more sympathetic attitude to Nationalists in the North and the South. Again ordinary Protestants began to fear the idea of a united Ireland. They began to attack Catholic civil rights marchers and 'the Troubles' began.

Since 1970, many Unionists have looked back to the days of Carson when politicians and private armies joined together to fight for Ulster. Ian Paisley has set up a new hardline Democratic Unionist Party. The UVF and the UDA have been formed to carry on the tradition of Carson's original Ulster Volunteer Force.

SOURCE 7 — Ian Paisley looks back to Carson

Ian Paisley paraded 500 men from a private Protestant army today (6th February 1981). He said 'These men are ready to fight and die rather than accept an all-Ireland Republic. They are prepared to defend their province in the same way as Lord Carson and the men of the Ulster Volunteer Force!

(Report from the London 'New Standard', February 1981)

▶ *Why do modern Unionists look back to the example of Carson in 1912?*
▶ *After the outbreak of the Troubles in 1968-9, a Nationalist politician, Eddie McAteer, said 'We are all prisoners of history here'.*
What do you think he meant?
Do you think he is right?

One of the thousands of Unionist posters produced 1912-1914.

THE
NEW STANDARD
Friday, February 6, 1981. Price 12p. *Incorporating the* **Evening News**

500 men pledge to die rather than see Ireland united

Protestants oppose the Anglo-Irish Agreement 1986.

BR

OR

POLITICIANS

	1880
1886 Ulster Unionist Party set up to fight Home Rule	1890
	1900
	1910
1912-3 Carson and Unionists prepare a provisional government for an independent Ulster	
	1920
1921-60 Hardline Unionist leaders run government of N. Ireland	
	1930
	1940
	1950
1963-8 Moderate Unionists discuss reforms for Catholics	
1968-9 Reforms rejected by extreme Unionists	1960
1971 Ian Paisley sets up a new, tough, Democratic Unionist Party	1970
1972 End of the Unionist controlled government	1980
1985 DUP oppose Anglo-Irish agreement	1990

closely linked 1800s - 1980s

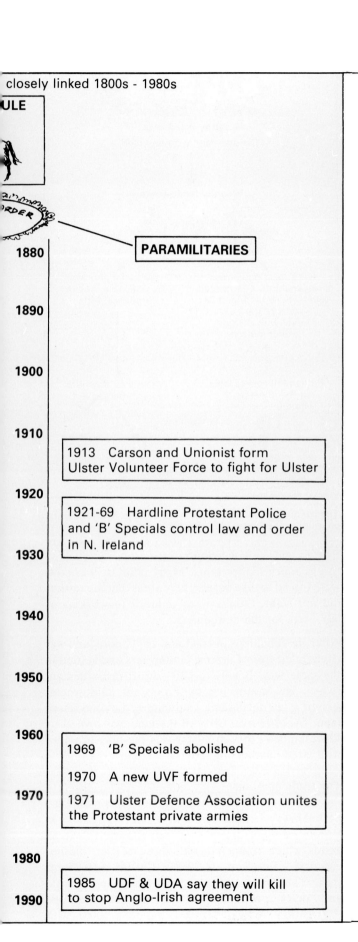

ULE

PARAMILITARIES

| 1880 |
| 1890 |
| 1900 |
| 1910 |

1913   Carson and Unionist form Ulster Volunteer Force to fight for Ulster

| 1920 |

1921-69   Hardline Protestant Police and 'B' Specials control law and order in N. Ireland

| 1930 |
| 1940 |
| 1950 |
| 1960 |

1969   'B' Specials abolished

1970   A new UVF formed

1971   Ulster Defence Association unites the Protestant private armies

| 1970 |
| 1980 |

1985   UDF & UDA say they will kill to stop Anglo-Irish agreement

| 1990 |

Protestants take to arms —
Carson's Ulster Volunteer Force 1914.

The armed B Specials combat the IRA in Northern Ireland 1920s.

The UDA on the march 1971 —
A modern version of Carson's UVF?

Economics

Today's conflict in Ireland is not only the result of political and religious factors. There are other factors involved. Of these the most important is economics — the business of money and making a living.

Economic problems and motives have played an important part in creating the three big splits which are at the root of today's conflict:

- the split between Catholic Nationalists and Protestant Unionists
- the split between North and South
- the split between Britain and the Irish Catholics.

Economics and the British conquest

Economic factors first played a part in the development of the conflict in the 16th century. When the British conquered Ireland they took control of the economy as well as the government. Then as now, power was about wealth — who had it and who didn't. In the 16th and 17th centuries the most powerful people were landowners and wealthy merchants.

The land question

In the 17th century the British government decided that, to stop rebellions in Ireland, they would have to put loyal subjects in power. So they started taking land from the native Irish (who were Catholic rebels) and giving it to Scottish and English settlers (who were loyal Protestants).

The first stage in this massive transfer of land was the 'Plantation' of Ulster in 1609. In 1607 the two main landowners in the province, the Earls of Tyrconnell and Tyrone, fled to France after they were implicated in a plot with Spain. Their lands were seized and sold off to wealthy English and Scottish landowners or merchants. They then let out their new land to

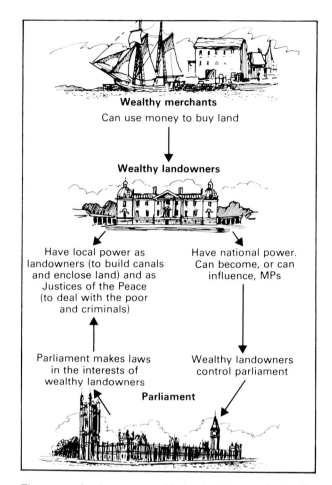

The connection between wealth, land and power. England's charmed circle in the 17th-18th centuries.

Wealthy merchants
Can use money to buy land

Wealthy landowners

Have local power as landowners (to build canals and enclose land) and as Justices of the Peace (to deal with the poor and criminals)

Have national power. Can become, or can influence, MPs

Parliament makes laws in the interests of wealthy landowners

Wealthy landowners control parliament

Parliament

A 19th century cartoon showing Irish peasants crushed by the cruel landlord. How useful is a biased source like this?

English and Scottish tenants or to Irish tenants willing to pay much higher rents. Many poor Irish tenants were forced to take barren, hilly areas that the settlers did not want. Others were reduced to working as labourers for the newcomers.

After the rebellions in 1641 and 1690 more land was confiscated from Catholic landowners and settled in the same way. Finally in 1704 the Irish Parliament (which was controlled by Protestant landowners) passed a law forbidding Catholics to buy any more land. By 1703 over 80% of the land was owned by Protestants — though Ulster was the only province with large numbers of settlers.

The trade question

As well as taking land, the British government also passed laws controlling Ireland's trade. As a colony in Britain's empire, Ireland was not allowed to export goods which competed with those of the 'mother country'. Between 1650-80 Cattle Acts kept Ireland's most important exports (sheep, pigs, cattle and dairy produce) out of English markets. 'Navigation Acts' destroyed Ireland's trade with America and the West Indies.

Economics and the fight for independence

The British government's plans for peaceful rule in Ireland came to nothing. After 1790 there was a long period of unrest in Ireland including several rebellions.

▶ *Look at the sources on this page.*
  What were the economic motives for this unrest?

The trade question

By 1780 the British parliament had removed all curbs on Irish trade. Despite this, bitterness and suspicion about the trade question still lingered on into the 1790s.

SOURCE 1 — Why Irishmen should rebel, 1790

We are ruled by Englishmen who care only about the trade of their own country. We have every resource for trade and manufacture, mines, navigable rivers and harbours — but all in vain. England starves our manufacturers. England sacrifices our rights to her lust for gold and power. If Ireland were free, her trade and manufactures would spring up like an air balloon and leave England far behind.

(Wolfe Tone, Revolutionary Nationalist, 1790)

The land question

By the beginning of the 19th century, the real economic grievance was land. The Irish Catholics deeply resented the loss of their lands and the harsh treatment they often got from new landlords. When Daniel O'Connell and the Parliamentary Nationalists looked for support, they soon got the backing of the discontented Catholic peasants. By the 19th century many farms had been divided and had become very small. Some landlords evicted tenants to make bigger holdings, and this caused even more bitterness on the part of the Catholics.

SOURCE 2 — An early nationalist looks for support

The landlords do not now and never did belong to this island. Tyrants they have been since first they set foot on our soil. I say that the soil of a country belongs to the people of that country, not to any one class.

(Fintan Lalor, 'The Irish Felon', 1848)

After the Famine many Protestant landlords evicted the Catholic tenants to increase the value of their land.
What do you think this evicted Catholic family felt about British justice?

The Great Famine and the Land War

Catholic resentment of their treatment by Protestant landlords was greatly increased by the Great Famine 1845-1849. About a million Irish people died of starvation and more emigrated.

SOURCE 1 — The Great Famine and the landlords, 1848

People whose land is in the keeping of others are not safe. The Irish Famine of '46 is proof. The corn crops were sufficient to feed the island. But the landlords would have their rents in spite of the famine and fever. They took the whole harvest and left hunger to their tenants. Had the people of Ireland been the landlords of Ireland, not a single human creature would have died of hunger.

(Fintan Lalor, 'The Irish Felon', 1848)

SOURCE 2 — Land War Poster, 1881

THE LAND WAR!
NO RENT!
NO LANDLORDS GRASSLAND

Tenant Farmers, now is the time. Now is the hour. You proved false to the first call made upon you.
REDEEM YOUR CHARACTER NOW.

NO RENT
UNTIL THE SUSPECTS ARE RELEASED.

The man who pays Rent (whether an abatement is offered or not) while PARNELL, DILLON &c., are in Jail, will be looked upon as a Traitor to his Country and a disgrace to his class.
No RENT, No Compromise, No Landlords' Grassland,
Under any circumstances.
Avoid the Police, and listen not to spying and deluding Bailiffs.
NO RENT! LET THE LANDTHIEVES DO THEIR WORST!
THE LAND FOR THE PEOPLE!

A Nationalist poster of 1881 — What are tenants asked to do to play their part in the Land War?

Evictions continued after the Famine, and so did the anger of the Catholic peasants. In 1879 a Fenian revolutionary, Michael Davitt, founded the Land League. Between 1879 and 1882 the Land League organised a campaign of intimidation and violence in the Irish countryside to win a better deal for poor tenant farmers.

SOURCE 3 — The Land League and the English Prime Minister.

Gladstone gives a new deal to Irish tenants 1881.

▶ *Why does the cartoonist think that the Prime Minister is producing a new land bill for Ireland?*

Unrest brings land reforms

In the late 19th century British politicians decided that reforms were needed in the Irish countryside, in order to stop the unrest. Between 1870 and 1903 various laws were passed that gave greater protection to tenants, and helped many thousands of them to buy their farms from their Protestant landlords.

By the outbreak of World War I, Catholics had won back control of much of the land taken from their ancestors in the 17th century. In 1870 they had owned 3% of the land; by 1916 this figure had risen to 64%.

British politicians hoped that this economic change would reduce support for the Nationalists. This did not happen. In the 20th century Catholic farmers have often supported anti-British Nationalists.

▶ *Why do you think this has happened?*

Economics, Unionists and Partition 1880-1920

A Belfast shipyard 1900: Protestant businessmen grew rich through their links with Britain. How did this affect the growth of Unionism?

In the 1790s, economic grievances had led a few Protestants to demand Irish independence. By the end of the 19th century most Ulster Protestants no longer wanted Ireland to become independent of Britain. In the 1880s they set up the Ulster Unionist party to fight to keep Ireland's links with Britain. It was the fierce opposition of Unionist politicians and private armies in 1912-14 which made the British government decide that Ireland would have to be divided into two.

Look at the evidence on this page.

▶ *What economic motives persuaded the Unionists to oppose a Dublin parliament in 1912-14?*

SOURCE 4 — Belfast factory owners oppose Home Rule, 1893

As part of the UK we have shared in the progress of industry in the great centres of England. How would our commercial interests be represented in a parliament in Dublin? We all know Ireland is an agricultural country. We are not prepared to come under the rule of a Dublin parliament dominated by poor farmers.

(from a statement by Belfast industrialists, 1893)

SOURCE 5 — Belfast under the Union, c. 1900

Belfast has done very well under the Union. Her population has quadrupled in 50 years. Her wage rates are higher than anywhere in Ireland. As to customs revenue, she ranks as the third port in the UK after London and Liverpool. She has the largest weaving factory, the largest shipping output, the largest tobacco factory and the largest ropeworks in the world.

(adapted from Thomas Sinclair 'The Liberal-Unionist case against Home Rule', c. 1900)

SOURCE 6 — Ulster's Solemn League and Covenant against Home Rule, September 1912

Being convinced that Home Rule would be disastrous to the material well-being of Ulster, as well as the whole of Ireland, subversive of our political and religious freedom . . . We men of Ulster pledge to stand by one another in defending our position in the United Kingdom.

Economics and divisions in the North 1920-72

During the years 1921-72 Northern Ireland was ruled by the Ulster Unionist Party as a separate state within the United Kingdom. Throughout this time economics continued to divide the two communities. Finally in 1968-9 fighting broke out once again between Protestant Unionists and Catholic Nationalists.

Look at the evidence on this page.

▶ *What economic grievances led to the outbreak of fighting in 1968-9?*

SOURCE 1 — Catholic workers forced out of the Belfast Shipyards, 1920

On 17th July Colonel Smyth of the Royal Irish Constabulary was murdered by the IRA. His assassination caused an outbreak of fury in the North. The worst trouble was in Belfast. Many Protestant shipyard workers (who had joined the army) found on their return from the war that their jobs had been taken by Catholics (who had stayed at home). When these Catholics openly supported Sinn Fein it only needed an incident such as this murder to bring matters to a head.

On July 21, a meeting of Belfast Unionist workmen decided to expel all Catholics from the shipyards. Serious attacks were made on them. Several were assaulted; others thrown into the harbour.

(adapted from Arthur Hezlet, 'The B-Specials', 1972)

SOURCE 2 — An Ulster politician discriminates, 1933

Many of you employ Catholics but I have not one about the house. In Northern Ireland the Catholic population is increasing. 97% of Catholics in Ireland are disloyal and disruptive. If we allow Catholics to work on our farms we are traitors to Ulster.

(Basil Brooke, Minister of Agriculture in Northern Ireland, 12 July 1933)

SOURCE 3 — A Unionist offers privileges to Protestants, 1961

Registers of unemployed Loyalists should be kept by the Unionist Party. The Unionist Party should make it clear that Loyalists have the first choice of jobs.

(Robert Babington, Unionist Party Candidate, 1961)

Catholic slums 1955.

SOURCE 4 — The economic demands of the Civil rights marchers, 1968-9

The economic demands of the Civil Rights marchers 1968-1969.

▶ *Why would Protestant Unionists oppose these demands?*

SOURCE 5 — A Nationalist explains why he joined the IRA in the 1970s

Most of my life I have been brought up as a Nationalist. However I grew up in a situation of such degradation and unemployment that the life our people lived was no life at all. I said to myself — when I grow up and get married I will want something better for my children than this.

(quoted by Sean Cronin, 'Irish Nationalism', 1980)

Economics and today's conflict

Since the British government began direct rule in 1972 they have tried to stop employers discriminating against Catholics. In 1976 they set up the Fair Employment Agency to check up on any discrimination.

SOURCE 6 — Fair Employment agency report into Belfast engineering firms, 1982

Firm	Protestant employees	Catholic employees
Sirocco	98%	2%
Shorts	92-96%	4-8%
Mackies	90%	10%
Ford	91%	9%
Harland & Wolff[1]	100% (skilled engineers)	—

[1] In 1985 Harland & Wolff received £36.5m of British government money.

▶ *Has the British government managed to stop job discrimination?*

Today Ulster has other serious economic problems which affect both communities, although Catholics tend to be more badly affected than Protestants.

▶ *Look at graph. What are these problems?*

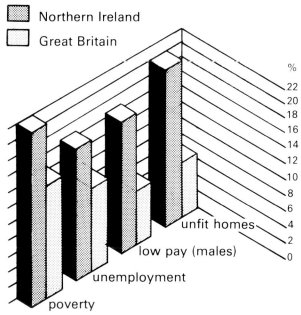

The disadvantages of living in Ulster 1982.

The unemployment rate has always been higher in Ulster than in the rest of the United Kingdom. Both sides have suffered but unemployment has been higher in Catholic areas:

1985 Average unemployment rate	21%
Rate in Derry and Strabane (Catholic areas)	42%

Since 1972 the British government has spent millions of pounds to create jobs both in private industry and in the public sector.

▶ *Look at the graph. How successful have they been?*

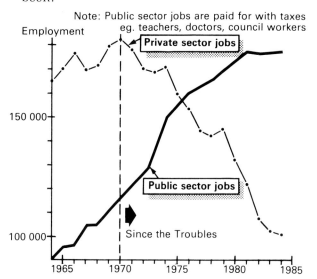

Changes in the economy of Ulster — The collapse of private industry.

Ulster has also become heavily dependent on British government money to pay for basic social services.

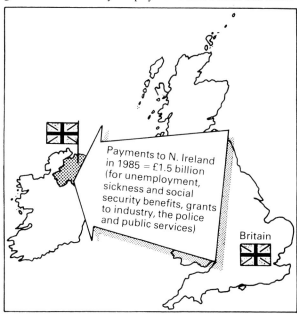

Ulster's British Lifeline 1985.

▶ *How have these economic problems helped to keep up tension between the two communities?*

▶ *Extreme Unionists keep threatening to cut all links between Ulster and Britain. What problems would Ulster people face if Unionists carried out this threat?*

▶ *Why might Ulster's economic problems make people in the South less keen to see a united Ireland?*

Social life

As well as political, religious and economic causes there are also social causes of today's conflict in Ireland. These are connected with the way people carry on their everyday lives at home and at school.

Separate schools

Today, the two communities are not only divided by religion and politics, they also go to separate schools.

Like other causes of the conflict, the idea of separate schools has a long history. In 1700 after their victory at the Battle of the Boyne, Protestants passed a series of 'Penal Laws' against Catholics. One of them banned Catholic teachers and carried a penalty of life imprisonment.

For over 100 years the only legal schools were those run by the Protestant churches. Catholics ran illegal 'hedge' schools for their children. Then, in 1831, the British government provided money to pay for schools for both groups. The government wanted these schools to have both Catholic and Protestant pupils, but the churchmen on both sides insisted on separate schools. When Northern Ireland was set up in the 1920s another attempt was made to have 'mixed' religion schools for all children. Again this was wrecked by churchmen on both sides.

Since 1974 many teachers have tried to bring pupils from separate schools together. Today many Catholic and Protestant students do 'History 13-16', and use this same book, about 'Conflict in Ireland'.

Look at the evidence on this page.

▶ *Why do you think Churchmen on both sides have continued to want separate schools?*
▶ *How was history teaching used in schools?*
▶ *How did separate schools help to cause today's conflict in Ireland?*
▶ *How could 'History 13-16' help to prevent future conflict in Ireland?*

SOURCE 1 — A Protestant education in the 1930s

Our schools drummed into us the Protestant story. On leaving school I had no notion of the past other than a few dreary details about our Protestant faith, the darkness of Rome and, for comic relief, intimate details of the Popes' private lives. We knew nothing of the Catholic world. That Catholics were allowed to live in London with our Protestant King seemed impossible.

(adapted from R. Harbinson, 'No Surrender', 1961)

SOURCE 2 — A Protestant grammar school 1950s

The teachers liked to pretend it was a civilised outpost of England: rugby, cricket and English headmasters. There was little to suggest we were living in Ireland — no Irish history, no Irish literature, no Irish music. I could rhyme off the names of the English Kings and Queens but I hardly even heard of Wolfe Tone and Daniel O'Connell.

(N. Longley, 'New Statesman', 1974)

SOURCE 3 — A Catholic grammar school in the 1960s

St. Patrick's Academy Dungannon, where I went, was a patriotic school. It owed its proudly Irish slant to the vice-Principal, Mother Benignus. She disliked the English. All her family had suffered at the hands of the British forces. She was very keen about Irish culture which did drive lots of people away who couldn't take it for breakfast, dinner and tea. She didn't hate Protestants. But her view was that you couldn't very well put up with them, they weren't Irish.

We learned Irish history. The interpretations we were given were very different from Protestant history books.

(Bernadette Devlin, 'The Price of My Soul', 1969)

A modern cartoonist's light-hearted view of a hedge-school. How realistic is it?

Divided even by sport — only Catholics play Gaelic games like this.

Separate housing areas.

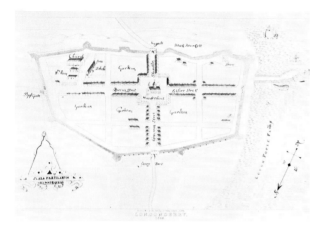

Derry 1625 — the walled city was, and is, a Protestant area. Catholics had to live outside by the bog side.

Derry 300 years on — Catholic slum housing in the "Bogside" 1970s.

Separate housing

In the cities of Belfast and Derry, most Catholics and Protestants live in separate areas. In Derry this goes back to the time of the Protestant Plantations in the early 17th century. Derry was given to a Company of London merchants. They rebuilt and fortified the town, renaming it Londonderry. Catholics had to live outside the walls 'by the bogside'. Today's Derry's Bogside district is a stronghold of the Nationalists.

In Belfast separate areas grew up in the early 19th century when the growing shipbuilding and linen industries attracted many Catholic workers. The first riots in Belfast between Catholics and Protestants began in 1832. Others have followed at intervals up to the present day.

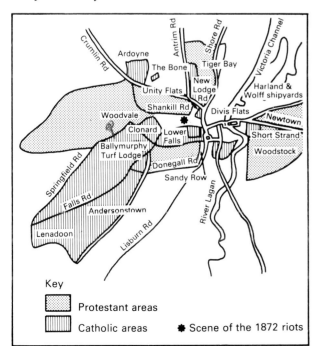

Key

▨ Protestant areas

▥ Catholic areas   ✳ Scene of the 1872 riots

The Catholic and Protestant ghettoes of Belfast — the scene of countless riots for the last hundred years.

SOURCE 4 — Falls v Shankill, 1872

The two sides met for a battle in the brick fields between the Shankill and Falls Road. The police tried in vain to separate them and the military were sent for. The houses on the Shankill Road have been gutted by mobs. Protestants living in Catholic areas and Catholics living in Protestant districts have found it necessary to change their quarters.

('Illustrated London News', 15 August 1872)

SOURCE 5 — A Catholic in a Loyalist area, 1970s

As he turned into his street he felt the eyes on him. He could not bear to look up and see the flutter of the Union Jacks and the Ulster flag. Of late there were more and more of these appearing in the estate. It was a dangerous sign that the Loyalists were getting angry. The flags should all have been down now because 12th July was long past.

Even looking at his feet Cal couldn't avoid the repulsion because the kerbstones had been painted red, white and blue. Cal felt that it was aimed at them, the McCluskeys, because his father and he were the only Catholic family left in the whole estate. Fear had driven the others out but his father would not move. 'No Loyalist bastard is going to drive me out of my home. They can kill me first'.

(from 'Cal', a novel by B. MacLaverty, 1983)

▶ *How do you think separate housing has helped to cause today's conflict in Ireland?*

▶ *Why do you think Unionists and Nationalists today are reluctant to live in the same areas?*

▶ *Can you think of another country where two groups of people live in separate areas and go to separate schools. Why has 'separate development' caused conflict there?*

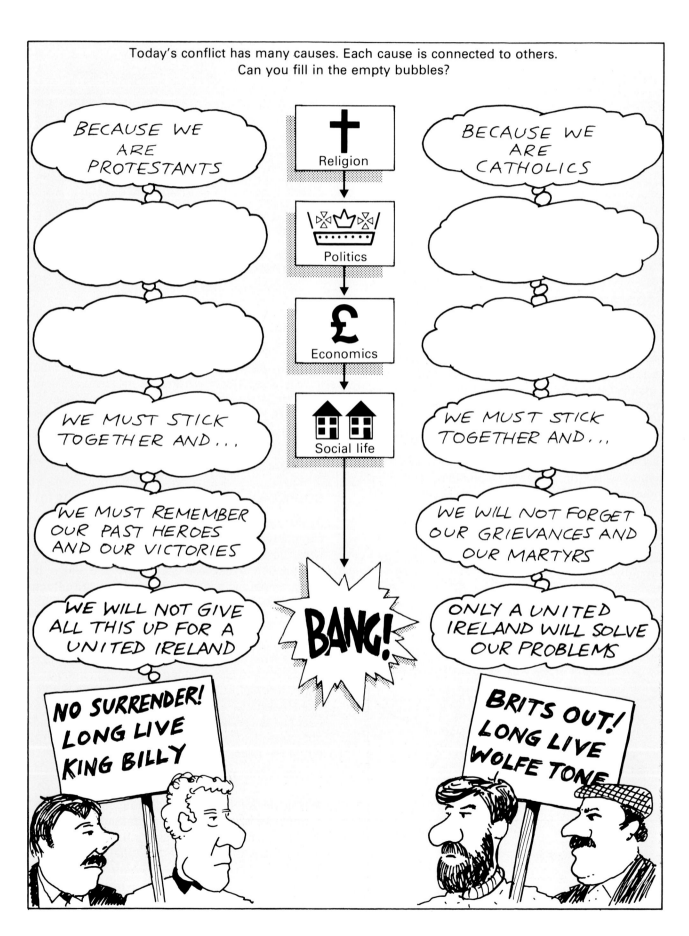

Turning points

We now know that:

- there are many causes of the present troubles in Ireland — social and economic, religious and political.
- these causes are closely connected with each other.
- these causes have roots which go a long way back into Ireland's past.

But when we investigate the causes of modern world conflicts we also ask other questions:

What are the short term causes of the conflict?
Was the present conflict inevitable?

▶ *Just because a conflict has many interconnecting causes, does it have to work out in one particular way?*
▶ *Is history a subject like physics which has 'laws' determining the way people/objects behave in given situations?*
▶ *Or in past conflicts have there been turning points along the way where people could have made different decisions and where events could have taken a different course?*

A turning point is a time of change when events or decisions happen which affect the future development of a problem. As a result the problem may be solved or it may continue.

These sections deal with six important turning points along the road to today's Irish Conflict. They have long-term as well as short-term causes.

When studying these turning points, think about these questions:

▶ *Why did it happen when it did — what short term causes can we see?*
▶ *What were the motives of the people involved?*
▶ *Could they have made a different decision?*
▶ *Why didn't things work out as people intended?*

Turning Points in modern Irish history. Could things have worked out differently?

Turning point 1: The triumph of Sinn Fein 1918

From 1800-1914 the Revolutionary Nationalists had looked like losers. Their rebellions had been crushed and ordinary Catholics had refused to support their aims or their methods. Instead Catholics had supported the political leaders of the Irish Nationalist Party and their peaceful campaign for an Irish parliament.

Suddenly in 1918 all this changed. In the General Election the majority of Irish Catholics voted for Sinn Fein, the Revolutionary Nationalist Party. Sinn Fein now had 73 MPs and the Irish Nationalist Party just six MPs. The Revolutionaries had triumphed at last. This shift in public opinion made a big difference to the future of Ireland.

Large crowds turn out to support John Redmond, the Irish Party leader in 1914. Soon they were to desert him.

▶ *Why did it happen?*

Historians have suggested several possible causes:

● The 'Irish Ireland' movement.
● Unionists opposition to Home Rule.
● Irish Nationalist Party involvement in the First World War.
● The 1916 Easter Rising.
● The Conscription crisis 1918.

▶ *How did these causes lead to the triumph of Sinn Fein?*
▶ *Were all the causes equally important?*
▶ *Was the collapse of the Irish Party and the victory of Sinn Fein inevitable? Or could things have worked out differently?*

To answer these questions we need to look in detail at each of the five causes.

Using an Irish book produced in 1922 — how can you tell the artist was interested in Ireland's Gaelic past?

1 The 'Irish Ireland' Movement

In the late 19th century many people became interested in Ireland's Gaelic past. They felt that Ireland was getting too much like England, and that the Irish language and Irish games should be used in place of ideas imported from Britain. The call for a more 'Irish Ireland' led to the development of new political ideas. These questioned the need for any sort of link between Ireland and Britain. In 1905 a Dublin journalist, Arthur Griffith, founded a political party called 'Sinn Fein' (which means 'Ourselves Alone'). Griffith wanted all Irish MPs to leave the House of Commons and set up an independent Irish parliament in Dublin.

Look at the following sources.

▶ *How important was all this before 1914?*

SOURCE 1 — The 'Irish Ireland' movement and its effect

All this had little political impact. Neither Irish speakers nor hurley players not even poets were going to break the connection with England.

(J. Bowyer Bell, 'The Secret Army', 1970)

SOURCE 2 — Sinn Fein's impact before 1914

Sinn Fein attracted many young republicans, and people who were disappointed with Home Rule. In 1908 Sinn Fein fought a by-election against a Home Ruler. The party was defeated and declined after that but Griffith did not give up hope.

(M. E. Collins, 'Ireland - Three', 1972)

2 Ulster Unionists' opposition to Home Rule

The aim of the Parliamentary Nationalists was to win Home Rule. This meant a separate parliament for the whole of Ireland based in Dublin and controlled by the Catholic majority.

In 1912 the Liberal Prime Minister, Asquith, brought in the Third Home Rule Bill which was due to become law in 1914.

The Irish Party leader, John Redmond, was delighted with the progress of Home Rule in 1912. His party seemed to have finally achieved its aim. Unfortunately for Redmond the Ulster Unionists, led by Edward Carson, declared that they would fight rather than accept Home Rule. The Ulster Volunteer Force was set up to back up this threat. By 1914 Redmond had reluctantly agreed that Ulster should be allowed to opt out of a Dublin parliament. When the First World War broke out in August 1914 the British declared that a final decision on Irish independence would have to wait until the end of the war.

▶ *How do you think this Unionist opposition affected support for Redmond and the Irish party after the war?*

3 The Irish Party and the War

There were two private armies in Ireland in 1914. Nationalists formed the Irish Volunteers as a counter to the UVF. The Volunteers were a mixture of Parliamentary and Revolutionary Nationalists. When the War began John Redmond urged Volunteers to join the British Army. 80,000 Catholic Volunteers served with the British army — many of them died in the trenches in France.

Look at sources 3 and 4.

▶ *How did Redmond's support for the British war effort help to bring about his defeat in the 1918 election?*

SOURCE 3 — The impact of the War on Irish Catholics

The English have got all they wanted from Ireland and don't care two pence about her feelings. The people are full of indignation but are powerless. It almost makes me cry to think of Irish soldiers fighting not for Ireland but for Carson and what he stands for. Home rule is dead and buried and the Irish Party is a tool of the British Empire. What the future holds in store for us God knows. There is a great revulsion of feeling in Ireland.

(from a letter by the Catholic Bishop of Killaloe, June 1915. The Bishop had previously supported the Irish Party.)

The Ulster Unionists pledged to fight Home Rule. How could this damage the Parliamentary Nationalists?

SOURCE 4 — The British War Cabinet

In May 1915 Asquith formed a coalition government bringing together Liberals and Conservatives and including Carson as Attorney General. The inclusion of the Ulster Unionist leader in the government was a blow to Redmond and the Nationalists — almost a slap in the face. The heart went out of the Irish Party.

(C. L. Mowat, 'The Irish Question in British Politics', 1966)

4 The Easter Rising 1916

A Fenian group, the Irish Republican Brotherhood, decided that the War was a good opportunity to stage an armed uprising against the British. Their leader, Patrick Pearse, had been deeply influenced by the Irish Ireland movement and he despised the Irish Party.

When Redmond showed his support for the British war effort, the revolutionary nationalists left the Irish Volunteers and set up their own rival force. Pearse planned to use these men in a rebellion.

The rising started on Easter Monday when the rebels seized control of the centre of Dublin. From the steps of the General Post Office, Pearse declared that the rebels were 'the provisional government of the Irish Republic'. The British forces soon surrounded the rebels who were hopelessly outnumbered.

After six days of fighting Pearse surrendered. The British army, under General Maxwell, executed fifteen of the leaders.

Sinn Fein had not been involved in the organisation of the Easter Rising but afterwards it gained many new recruits. Survivors of the rebellion, such as Eamon de Valera, added a new strength to the party.

Throughout 1917 Sinn Fein grew more powerful. For the first time it defeated Irish Party Candidates in several by-elections.

Look at sources 5-7.
▶ *Why did the Easter Rising lead to increased support for Sinn Fein?*
▶ *How could the British government have prevented this?*

SOURCE 5 — An Irish Party MP criticises British policy after the Easter Rising

You are washing out our whole life's work in a sea of blood. Thousands of people in Dublin, who ten days ago were bitterly opposed to the whole of the Sinn Fein movement and to the rebellion, are now becoming infuriated against the government on account of these executions.

(John Dillon speaking to the House of Commons, 11 May 1916)

SOURCE 6 — The Rising and an Irish soldier in the British Army

In 1916 I was in Mesopotamia (Iraq) with the British Expeditionary Force. Outside the orderly room I saw a notice. It told us of this rising in Dublin, and the executions of men I'd never heard of — I said to myself, 'What the hell am I doing with the British army? It's with the Irish I should be!'

(Tom Barry, later a commander of the IRA, speaking in 'Curious Journey', 1982)

SOURCE 7 — Who organised the Easter Rising?

The newspapers and the public called it the 'Sinn Fein' rebellion. Although Sinn Fein had had nothing to do with it, so little was known of the Rising's real leaders and their motives that a link with Sinn Fein seemed the only explanation.

(Robert Kee, 'Ireland: a history', 1980)

The impact of the Easter Rising —

The rebel leaders were executed. What was the effect of the executions?

5 Conscription 1918

By March 1918, the British were running short of men in the war with Germany. The government decided to bring in conscription in Ireland: this meant that Irish men would be forced to join the British Army.

Look at the sources 8-10.
▶ *How did conscription help Sinn Fein to win in the 1918 election?*

SOURCE 8 — The impact of the conscription crisis

No-one who had not been in Ireland during the past six weeks can possibly realise how passionate is the resentment which has been aroused by conscription. Men are ready to take to the hills or die fighting in their homes rather than be compelled to join the Army. The tension is extraordinary.

(Hugh Law, an Irish Party MP, June 1918)

SOURCE 9 — Sinn Fein and conscription

The only recent result of conscription had been to give a tremendous fillip to Sinn Fein, so that during the year the number of members grew from 66,270 to 120,080. The conscription threat was, indeed, second only to the executions of the Easter week leaders in creating a substantial backing for Sinn Fein among the Irish people.

(Edgar Holt 'Protest in Arms', 1960)

SOURCE 10 — Catholics make a national pledge

Look at the document below.
▶ *How can we tell that these people were influenced by the Irish Ireland movement?*
▶ *Which important group of Irish people began to support Sinn Fein and the Revolutionary Nationalists for the first time?*

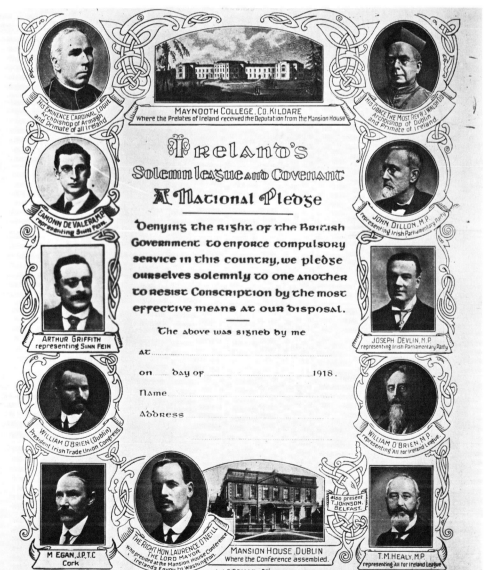

The anti-conscription oath of April 1918 won the backing of the Catholic Church for the Revolutionary Nationalists. How can we tell this?

Turning point 2: Dividing Ireland 1920-21

The Irish War of Independence

After the 1918 election most Irish MPs were members of Sinn Fein, and they wanted a complete break with Britain. In January 1919 these MPs set up their own parliament in Dublin, the Dail Eireann. This declared itself the government of an independent Irish Republic. Soon after, the survivors of the Easter Rising were reorganised as the Irish Republican Army (IRA).

For most of 1919 there was an uneasy peace. Then in 1920 the IRA began a guerrilla war against the Royal Irish Constabulary. The RIC were armed and still controlled by the British. The IRA staged surprise attacks on police stations and patrols. Suspected police informers were shot. The British sent reinforcements for the RIC recruited from the English unemployed. The new recruits were called 'The Black and Tans' because of the colour of their makeshift uniform. The Black and Tans soon won a reputation for great brutality. IRA suspects were beaten and sometimes killed. After an IRA attack the Black and Tans often burned down the houses of local Catholics.

Ulster goes it alone

By 1920 British rule in Ireland was collapsing. The only part not controlled by Sinn Fein and the IRA was Ulster. Here the Protestant private army, the Ulster Volunteer Force (UVF), was ready to fight to keep the North out of an independent Ireland.

The British government tried to end the crisis by dividing the six most Protestant counties of Ulster from the rest of Ireland. The two parts, Northern and Southern Ireland, were to stay part of the United Kingdom but they were also to be given their own local parliaments. The Northern Unionists reluctantly accepted the new arrangements. Sinn Fein rejected them. The guerrilla war continued.

The Dail Eireann in session.

Black and Tans on the lookout for rebels.

Black and Tans drilling.

A row of houses burnt by Black and Tans in Balbriggan, 1921.

The peace talks

By the summer of 1921 there was a stalemate in the war. Neither side was close to victory. In July 1921 a truce was arranged. Sinn Fein leaders were invited to London to talk about a peace treaty between the Nationalists and the British.

Between July and December 1921 three groups were involved in tense negotiations about the future of Ireland: the British, the Nationalists and the Ulster Unionists. The chart on p. 70 shows their views at the start of these talks.

Neither the British nor the Nationalists got what they really wanted. Instead they signed a peace treaty which kept Ireland divided and gave the Nationalists their own government in the South, which remained within the British Empire.

▶ *Look at the evidence on the following pages. It shows:*

i. *The attitudes of the leaders who made the decisions for each group:*

British government:	*David Lloyd George*
	Austen Chamberlain
	Bonar Law
Nationalists:	*Arthur Griffith*
	Eamon de Valera
Unionists:	*James Craig*

ii. *Some of the factors which influenced their decision.*

Then try and answer the key question:

Why did things not work out as the British, Nationalists and Unionists hoped?

	BRITISH	NATIONALISTS	UNIONISTS
What they wanted	**First choice**: a reunited Ireland with one parliament in Dublin which had close links with Britain and the Empire **Second best**: accept that Ireland would stay divided with two separate parliaments in Belfast and Dublin both closely linked to Britain	**First Choice**: a reunited Ireland free of all links with Britain, called 'The Irish Republic' ruled from Dublin **Second best**: accept the partition of Ireland but aim to win back control of the North in the future	**First choice**: keep Ulster separate from the South but united with Britain **Second best**: Ulster to stay separate from the South but with its own parliament
How they would get it	If negotiations failed the British army would have to force Ulster to accept a united Ireland and crush the IRA to regain control of the South The British had to persuade the Nationalists to stop fighting and accept the partition of Ireland into two separate states	If negotiations failed the Nationalists would have to start up their guerrilla war and defeat both the British and the Unionists Sinn Fein leaders would have to persuade the IRA to give up their fight for a united Ireland	The Unionists were ready to fight if the British tried to force them into an independent state ruled from Dublin

THE KINDEST CUT OF ALL.

∧ British cartoon from 1920 showing Prime Minister Lloyd George cutting up Ireland. Why do you think he was nicknamed the "Welsh Wizard"?

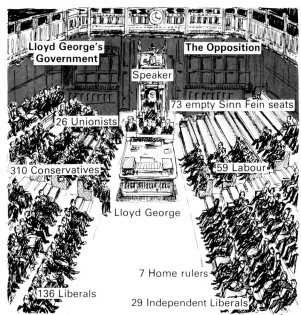

The British House of Commons 1920-21.

The British government - decision makers

David Lloyd George

Lloyd George had been Prime Minister since 1916. He had few fixed views on Ireland but he wanted to be known as the man who solved the Irish problem. Whatever the solution, he had to make sure that Ireland was no longer a threat to Britain's security as she had been in World War I (1914-18).

Lloyd George was a liberal and one of the most able and gifted politicians of the time. During the negotiations Lloyd George came up with an ingenious proposal: if the Unionists and Nationalists accepted partition as a temporary solution, a Boundary Commission would be set up later to decide if the boundary between North and South was fair.

Bonar Law, Austen Chamberlain

These were leaders of the Conservative Party. They had been friends and allies of Edward Carson, the Unionist leader who stood against 'Home Rule' in 1912. They were determined to protect the Ulster Unionists and keep Ireland in the British Empire.

Factors influencing their decision

SOURCE 1 — Lloyd George's Government in 1921

Lloyd George's was a coalition government. Some of the Conservative members were opposed to Irish Independence and had very close links with Ulster Unionists. On balance, it does seem that Lloyd George really was anxious to settle the Irish problem by setting up an All Ireland Parliament in Dublin. He took as hard a line with Craig as he dared, but he had sworn not to force Ulster into a united Ireland and he did not want civil war. Neither did he want divisions in his Cabinet.

(Carlton Younger, 'A State of Disunion', 1972)

SOURCE 2 — Memories of an earlier attempt to force Ulster into a United Ireland

In 1911 Carson threatened to set up a Provisional government in Ulster if the Home Rule Bill was passed, and the Unionists began organising a private army, the Ulster Volunteer Force. The Unionists had the full backing from the Conservative Party and the British army commanders.

In March 1914 when the Westminster government finally summoned up enough courage to stage a move against the Unionists, a brigadier and fifty-four officers at the Curragh military camp near Dublin mutinied rather than take part. The whole operation had to be called off.

(Michael Farrell, 'Northern Ireland — The Orange State', 1976)

SOURCE 3 — Sinn Fein rules the country, 1920

Sinn Fein rules the country — and rules it admirably. Crimes of any kind are dealt with by the Sinn Fein courts, who try the accused with perfect fairness. Missing property, if reported to the Sinn Fein police, is inevitably found and restored to the owners.

(letter from a Limerick landlord, 1920)

SOURCE 4 — The military strength of the British, 1921

Lloyd George had just been warned that Ireland could be reconquered only by a full-scale war and an army of 100,000 men.

(A. J. P. Taylor, 'English History 1914-1945', 1965)

SOURCE 5 — Lloyd George had other problems to worry about

The last two years of the Lloyd George's government (1920-22) were overshadowed by the trade slump, unemployment and the drive to cut government spending.

Demonstrations by the unemployed were organised by the National Unemployed Workers Movement. The NUWM was considered to be a Communist

The body of Terence MacSwiney, Mayor of Cork, who died on hunger strike in a British prison in 1920. Events like this won great sympathy for Irish Nationalists all over the world.

organisation. In October 1920 crowds of unemployed men seeking to see Lloyd George were charged upon by police and beaten about.

(C. L. Mowat, 'Britain between the Wars', 1956)

SOURCE 6 — Public opinion turns against Lloyd George and the Black and Tans

Labour Party's commission on Ireland, January 1921: 'Things are being done in the name of Britain which must make her name stink in the nostrils of the world'.

The Archbishop of Canterbury, February 1921: 'The government's policy is morally unjust. If you get peace by wrong-doing then you have not really won a peace that is worthwhile'.

SOURCE 7 — The pressure of public opinion

Lloyd George knew that British opinion, and that of the Empire and the United States, would rebel against any further bloodshed in Ireland. What he put forward was a gigantic bluff.

(G. Dangerfield, 'The Damnable Question', 1977)

Protests at the execution of IRA men captured during the War of Independence.

Irish Nationalists - decision makers

Eamon de Valera

Since 1919 de Valera had been the President of the Dail government. He was anxious for peace, but he was also determined to see an Irish Republic which included Ulster. He did not go to the negotiations in London but kept in close touch.

Eamon de Valera.

Arthur Griffith

Griffith was the founder of Sinn Fein and the leader of the Irish delegation to London. He hated violence and was more ready than de Valera to make a deal in order to stop the killing. His delegation were given authority to sign a treaty with the British on behalf of the Dail.

Arthur Griffith.

Factors influencing their decisions

SOURCE 8 — IRA estimates of armed men on both sides, 1920-1

IRA men on active service		5,000
IRA men in reserve		10,000
	total	15,000
British troops and police		65,000
Ulster Volunteer Force		20,000
B Specials		16,000
	total	101,000

SOURCE 9 — People in the South wanted peace

In the interval between the truce and the start of negotiations, the military situation had disintegrated for the Irish. Now that dangers were over, recruits flocked in for the IRA. These sunshine soldiers used their position to bully, to loot and to extort money. The old tight organisation had broken up. Whatever the ideas of the gunmen, the war would not be restarted. The mass of the people were content with the peace, and would give little help to the IRA. All the advantages would lie with the British forces, rested but not disbanded by the truce.

(from C. L. Mowat, 'Britain between the Wars', 1956)

British soldiers inspecting a bridge damaged by one of the IRA flying columns of guerrillas.

SOURCE 10 — de Valera's position

We cannot admit the right of the British government to mutilate our country. However we do not plan to use force against Northern Protestants.

(Eamon de Valera, July 1921)

SOURCE 11 — The Irish delegates and the Boundary Commission

Wisely or foolishly the Irish believed that the Boundary Commission must bring them two more counties and that the North would be made too small to carry on as a result.

(adapted from Frank Pakenham, 'The Treaty Negotiations', 1966)

SOURCE 12 — The strength of the negotiating teams

Lloyd George was one of the most brilliant political manipulators of all time. Only de Valera at the head of the Irish delegation might have been a match for Lloyd George. Ireland's best player was kept among the reserves.

(Robert Kee, 'The Green Flag', 1972)

The Ulster Unionists - decision makers

James Craig

In 1921 Craig replaced Edward Carson as the leader of the Ulster unionists. Like Carson, Craig had been involved in the Ulster Volunteer Force (UVF) before the First World War. Originally Craig had wanted to keep the whole of Ireland as part of the United Kingdom. In May 1921, however, Craig became the first Prime Minister of Northern Ireland. Although he did not go to the negotiations, the British were in constant contact with Craig. He had many friends in the Conservative Party.

James Craig.

Factors influencing decisions

SOURCE 13 — The Ulster Unionist attitude

During the negotiations Lloyd George wrote several letters to Sir James Craig proposing Irish unity, and guaranteeing the safety of the Unionists. But the attitude of the Government of Northern Ireland was, 'What we have we hold.'

(Maureen Wall, 'Partition — The Ulster Question', 1966)

Craig set up the B Specials — an armed Protestant police force.

SOURCE 14 — Carson's last warning to the British

If you are unable to protect us from the machinations of Sinn Fein, we will take the matter into our own hands. We will reorganise the Ulster Volunteers. These are not mere words.

(Carson's 'Battle of the Boyne' speech, 12 July 1920)

SOURCE 15 — James Craig and the Boundary Commission

Craig met Lloyd George on December 9th and told him that the Six Counties Government would give up none of their territory. The British Prime Minister reassured him on the boundary question. It was merely a matter of tidying up.

(Calton Younger, 'A State of Disunion', 1972)

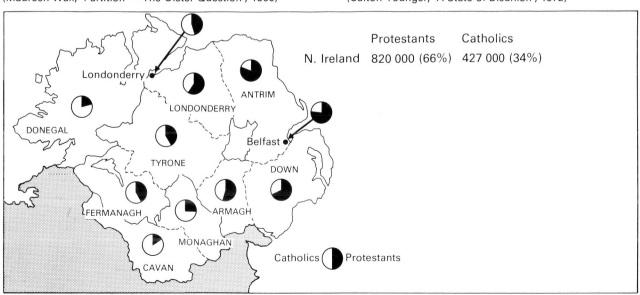

	Protestants	Catholics
N. Ireland	820 000 (66%)	427 000 (34%)

A map showing the proportion of Catholics and Protestants in the nine counties of Ulster in 1911.

Why were Unionists ready to abandon Donegal, Cavan and Monaghan?
Why were Nationalists in Tyrone and Fermanagh particularly angry at being included in Northern Ireland?

Turning point 3: The North explodes 1968

The present crisis in Northern Ireland began in 1968. Since then thousands have been killed or injured. At the time the outbreak of violence was unexpected. When O'Neill took control of the government of Ulster in 1963, it seemed that Catholics and Protestants were starting to bury their old differences. O'Neill promised changes for the Catholic minority. This pleased them but his reforms were slow in coming. So in 1967 a group of Catholics started the Civil Rights Movement. A year later they organised a series of marches and demonstrations in the hope of speeding up the reforms. It was during these marches that fighting first broke out between Catholics, Protestants and the police. This conflict has been going on ever since.

▶ *Why did the North explode after 40 years of uneasy peace?*
▶ *Who started the fighting?*
▶ *Why did it continue?*
▶ *What were the motives of the people involved?*
▶ *Is there a simple explanation?*

Looking for a simple explanation

Here are two explanations suggested by people at the time.

Explanation 1   The violence was all the fault of the IRA.

"What are you waiting for? All you have to do is ignore the others and go for the feller in the trench coat."
Is it all the fault of the IRA? What is the view of this cartoonist?

Look carefully at the following evidence.
▶ *Does it support or contradict this explanation?*
▶ *Who might believe this explanation and why?*

SOURCE 1 — The state of the IRA in 1967

In 1967 we called a meeting of local leadership throughout the country to assess the strength of the movement. We discovered we had no movement.

(Cathal Goulding, IRA leader)

SOURCE 2 — When did the IRA join the fight?

1962   IRA abandon their campaign of violence because of lack of Catholic support.
1963   O'Neill promises a fairer deal for Catholics.
1967   Civil rights movement starts.
1968   October — fighting breaks out during a march in Derry.
1969   January — fighting breaks out on a march at Burntollet Bridge.
       August — more fighting between Protestants and Catholics in Belfast. The British army moves in.
       December — IRA cannot agree what action to take. They split into groups: Officials and Provisionals.
1970   Provisionals begin bombing campaign.
1971   Provisionals begin to shoot British soldiers.

Derry, October 1968 — Protestant police attack Catholic Civil Rights marchers.

SOURCE 3 — Did the IRA start it?

The police view that they had on their hands an armed uprising led by the IRA was incorrect. There is no credible evidence that the IRA planned or organised the disturbances.

(From 'Report of Tribunal of Inquiry' by Justice Scarman for the British government, April 1972)

Explanation 2   It all started with the Catholics. They wanted to reunite North and South. This made the Protestants determined to oppose them.

A simple scientific formula for the outbreak of fighting. Catholic pressure for a united Ireland + Protestant resistance = violence.

Look at the evidence and answer these questions.
▶ *Does it support or contradict explanation 2?*
▶ *Who might believe it and why?*

A Protestant jumps a queue for council homes.

SOURCE 4 — The advantages and disadvantages of living in the North in the 1960s

The British Welfare state (developed after the war) increased family allowances and gave us a Health Service. These helped to shield Catholics from the worst effects of unemployment and poverty. Since such benefits were not available in the South, the idea of a united Ireland as the only way to make things better began to weaken.

The Education Act of 1944 gave Catholic working-class children the chance to go to grammar school and university. By the early 1960s we could easily get a place at a university but couldn't get a job as a lavatory cleaner at Derry Guildhall. That made us angry.

(adapted from Eamonn McCann, 'War and an Irish town', 1974. McCann was a leading member of the Civil Rights movement.)

Many Protestants were horrified when O'Neill visited Catholic schools. Why do you think they were so upset?

SOURCE 5 — Catholic Civil Rights marchers with their demands on their banners

Catholics demand a fair deal in Northern Ireland.

SOURCE 6 — Who inspired the Civil Rights marchers in 1968? A French connection

Why did the tinder which had lain around in a combustible state for so many years catch fire at this particular moment? The answer lies partly in the situation itself, but also in the rest of the world in 1968. 1968 was the year of the students' revolt. At French universities in May students brought France to a standstill.

(adapted from James Callaghan 'A House Divided', 1973. Callaghan was the British minister responsible for Northern Ireland.)

SOURCE 7 — American inspiration

In 1966 a meeting was held to discuss a Civil Rights movement for Northern Ireland like the one second-class black citizens of the United States had organised to demand their rights under the leadership of Martin Luther King.

(adapted from Robert Kee, 'Ireland — A History', 1980)

▶ *Who would have inspired the marchers if they had wanted a united Ireland?*

Looking for a more accurate explanation

Now look carefully at the next set of evidence. Then ask yourselves the same questions again:

▶ *Who started the fighting?*
▶ *Why did it continue?*
▶ *What were the motives of the people involved?*

Then try and work out a more accurate explanation for the outbreak of violence between Catholics and Protestants in 1968-9.

SOURCE 8 — Violence breaks out on a march in Derry, 5 October 1968

Our route was blocked by a cordon of police about three hundred yards from the starting point. We marched into the police cordon but failed to force a way through. We noticed another police cordon had cut us off from behind. There were no exits so we were trapped. The crowd milled round for a few minutes, no one knowing what to do.

The two police cordons moved simultaneously onto the crowd. Men, women and children were clubbed to the ground. About a hundred had to go to hospital for treatment.

(Eamonn McCann, 'War and an Irish town', 1974)

▶ *Is the answer simple or more complicated? Why?*
▶ *Look back at the Snatch Squad cartoon (p. 74). What other explanations does this suggest?*

SOURCE 10 — Fighting on a Civil Rights march, January 4 1969

Then we came to Burntollet bridge. From the lanes at each side of the road burst hordes of screaming people wielding bottles, iron bars, cudgels studded with nails. They waded into the march beating the hell out of everybody.

I saw a young fellow getting a thrashing from four or five of Ian Paisley's supporters with a policeman looking on. I went rampaging up the road saying not one policeman at Burntollet Bridge would live to be sorry for what he had done.

(Bernadette Devlin, 'The Price of My Soul', 1969. Devlin was a leading member of the Civil Rights movement.)

SOURCE 11 — The motives of Paisley and his followers

The O'Neillites were forsaking the past, letting Ulster's enemies take a hold on the country.

(A follower of Paisley speaking in 'Ulsters Uncertain Defenders', 1964)

Catholics man the barricades in the Battle of the Bogside, Derry, August 1969.

SOURCE 9 — The police visit a Catholic area, January 1969

The area was peaceful and deserted at 2 am when a mob of policemen came from the city centre shouting and singing:
  'Hey, hey we're the monkees,
  And we're going to monkey around,
  Till we see your blood flowing,
  All along the ground.'

They broke in windows with their batons, kicked doors and shouted to the people to 'come out and fight, you Fenian bastards'.

(Eamonn McCann, 'War and an Irish town', 1974)

SOURCE 12 — A British judge comments on the violence in 1968-9

Neither the IRA nor any Protestant organisation planned the riots. They arose from a complex political, social and economic situation. The events of 1968-9 convinced many Protestants that Catholics were trying to end the links between Northern Ireland and the United Kingdom. The same events made Catholics believe that the police were their enemy. There were six occasions during these riots when the police were seriously at fault.

(adapted from the 'Report of the Tribunal of Inquiry' by Justice Scarman, 1972)

Turning point 4: The fall of Stormont

Between 1921 and 1971 the real power in Northern Ireland lay with the Stormont government in Belfast. All this came to an end on 24 March 1972 when the British government suspended the Stormont parliament and began to rule Ulster direct from London. This marked the end of 50 years of Protestant control.

One explanation for the end of Stormont is that the local Protestant politicians could not stop the violence growing after 1968. The Stormont government tried to end the crisis in three ways:

1. They brought in reforms to make Northern Ireland fairer for Catholics.
2. They arrested hundreds of suspected terrorists and locked them up without a trial. This was called internment.
3. They used British soldiers to stop disorder on the streets.

None of these solutions worked. The Provisional IRA grew in strength and their campaign of bombing and shootings caused more and more casualties. Loyalist groups started to seek out and kill Catholic Nationalists.

▶ *Why did all these solutions fail?*
▶ *Was their failure inevitable?*
▶ *Could the British or Stormont governments have made them work? If so how?*

Solution 1: Reforms

Even before the arrival of the British army, the Stormont government had started to bring in reforms to meet the demands of Catholics. More followed. Look at the chart below:

▶ *Why were Catholics not satisfied with these reforms?*
▶ *Why were Protestants angered by these reforms?*
▶ *How could these reforms lead to violence?*

Catholic Complaints and Unionist Reforms 1969-71

Long-standing Catholic Criticisms	Response of the Ulster Unionist Government 1969-71
1. The armed B Specials were manned entirely by Protestants.	1. The B Specials were disbanded to be replaced by the Ulster Defence Regiment. The UDR was meant to be a mixed force but by November 1972 it was 96% Protestant.
2. People could be locked up without trial and mistreated in other ways under the Special Powers Act.	2. The government did not change the Special Powers Act.
3. Catholics found it more difficult than Protestants to get a vote in local elections.	3. Election rules were changed to treat all people equally.
4. Council boundaries were fixed or 'gerrymandered' to give unionist candidates a better chance of winning.	4. The government agreed to new, fair boundaries. They were not ready until May 1973.
5. Catholics were unable to share in government power.	5. One Catholic was brought into the Cabinet in October 1971.
6. Protestants found it easier to get good council houses.	6. A fair 'points system' was introduced for giving out council houses.

Paisley's followers called for the resignation of O'Neill.

Solution 2: Internment

The last Stormont Prime Minister was Brian Faulkner. He came to power in March, 1971, at a time when the Provos were mounting a massive bombing campaign. There were 304 explosions in Northern Ireland between January and July 1971. Faulkner made a fateful decision to stop the violence: he decided to bring in internment. This was meant to be used against all suspected terrorists — Protestants as well as Catholics.

Why did Faulkner introduce internment? As a young politician, he had helped to deal with the last outbreak of IRA violence 1956-62. Internment had been used then and it had worked. Faulkner tried to learn a lesson from history.

Faulkner's hope that 'history would repeat itself' proved disastrously wrong. In the months after internment the Provisional IRA went from strength to strength. The violence of some Catholics increased the fears of working-class Protestants. Loyalist vigilante groups gained new recruits; in September 1971 the Ulster Defence Association was formed. The Unionist politicians were losing control over both the Catholic and the Protestant communities.

Look at sources 1 and 2.
▶ *Why did internment fail to stop this happening?*

SOURCE 1 — The effects of internment

By mid December 1971, 1,576 people had been arrested by the army under the Special Powers Act — virtually all of them Catholic. That meant almost 1,576 families who had experienced the shock of arrest often in the early hours of the morning and without much tenderness.

(from a report by the Sunday Times 'Insight Team', 1972)

Anti-internment protest in London.

"My good fellow, you're allowed to scream only under torture! This is merely 'inhuman treatment' so pull yourself together".

A cartoon commenting on British treatment of internees.

SOURCE 2 — How internees were treated

Hooding — detainees were kept fully hooded except when interrogated or in rooms by themselves
Noise — when detainees were held together they were subjected to a continuous hissing noise
Sleep — it was the general policy to deprive men of sleep during the early days of the operation

(extract from the 'Compton Report', an official British government report, 1971)

Solution 3: The British Army

When British troops went into Northern Ireland there was rejoicing among many Catholics. They were not keen to see the return of the IRA and thought that the soldiers would protect them from Protestant violence. Catholics gave tea and sandwiches to the newly arrived British forces. This friendly atmosphere did not last long.

Look at sources 3-7.
▶ *What went wrong?*
▶ *How did the British Army help to bring about the fall of Stormont?*

At first many Catholics welcomed the British soldiers. Soon Catholic youths were fighting them. Why did this happen?

SOURCE 3 — The British Army

The Army was designed and trained to be aggressive.

(Taylor Downing, 'The Troubles', 1980)

Catholic graffiti.

SOURCE 4 — The Provos join the fray, Belfast 1970

On 27th June, 1970, for the first time, armed Provisionals appeared on the streets to challenge the UVF. The gun battle which followed lasted all night. There were five dead, four of them Protestants. The army's response was to get tough. On 3rd July a search for arms in Catholic areas led to allegations of damage to property by the soldiers. All the local people were forced by the Army to stay in their houses, this curfew lasted 36 hours. Four people were killed and the army's conduct ensured the hostility of the Catholic ghettoes.

(Taylor Downing, 'The Troubles', 1980)

SOURCE 5 — A Catholic gets into trouble

A Belfast docker, John Benson, painted 'No Tea Here' on the wall of his street — a reference to the practice of giving tea to the troops. The Army complained to the police. Deciding that the slogan was 'an obvious attempt to intimidate people', the magistrate gave Benson six months for breach of the peace.

(The Sunday Times Insight Team, 'Ulster', 1972)

SOURCE 6 — 'Bloody Sunday' January 1972: an eye witness remembers

In December 1971 the Northern Resistance movement (which was supported by the Provisionals) announced that, if internees were not released by Christmas, they would organise protest marches. The Civil Rights March in Derry on 30th January was one of these.

When the army started shooting that day the first reaction, after fear, was bewilderment. Why were they shooting? At Free Derry corner, where most people had gathered, the crowd flung themselves to the ground. Looking up one could see stragglers running panic stricken, bounding over the barricade, three of them crumpling to the ground. An hour and a half later no one knew for certain how many were dead. Some said three, some five. (It was actually thirteen.)

Later an IRA man said 'Our military orders after "Bloody Sunday" were to kill every British soldier we could'.

(Eamon McCann, 'War in an Irish town', 1974)

SOURCE 7 — The Army and the IRA

It was not long before occasional clumsy brutality on the part of the British forces provoked an angry reaction from the population. It was not difficult for an IRA, trying to control Catholic areas of Derry and Belfast, to use this reaction for their own ends.

(Robert Kee, 'Ireland — A History', 1980)

Bloody Sunday — the last straw. British troops opened fire on this Civil Rights march killing thirteen people.

Turning point 5: The failure of power sharing

Since the fall of Stormont in 1972, British leaders have tried to find a new system of government for Ulster which would satisfy everyone. So far they have tried two schemes for sharing power between the Catholic minority and the Protestant majority.

1   Power sharing executive 1974
In June 1973 the British government arranged fair elections for a Northern Ireland Assembly. The Unionist Party won most seats but they got together with the SDLP and agreed together on a plan for power sharing. This meant setting up a Northern Ireland Executive including Nationalists as well as Unionists. The Irish Republic took part in these talks and gave its backing to the Executive. It was also agreed to set up a Council of Ireland with representatives from the North and the South.

2   Northern Ireland Assembly 1982
In 1982 the British set up a new Northern Ireland assembly elected by fair voting. At first this was to have power of discussion only. But, if Catholics and Protestants could agree on any problem, they were to be given the power to deal with it.

Both schemes failed. The 1974 power sharing plan was abandoned after four months because of bitter opposition from ordinary Protestants. The 1982 Assembly plan did not work either. Catholics refused to go. Protestants turned up but said they wanted no part in a new power sharing deal. At this time many Catholics deserted the SDLP and turned to Sinn Fein, the Revolutionary Nationalists. Sinn Fein have no intention of making British solutions work. Today the gap between Unionists and Nationalists is as wide as ever.

▶ *Why have the British failed to get support from ordinary Catholics and Protestants for their peace plans?*
▶ *Could things have worked out differently?*

Below is material on two important events closely connected with the failure of power sharing.

The Ulster workers strike 1974

The Power Sharing Executive took over on January 1 1974 headed by Unionist leaders, Brian Faulkner, and SDLP leader Gerry Fitt. Even before they began work they were widely condemned by sections of the Protestant community.

Look at sources 1 and 2.
▶ *Why were many Protestants so opposed to power sharing?*

SOURCE 1 — Ian Paisley's attitude to power-sharing

Catholics don't want a share in the government of Northern Ireland. They want Northern Ireland to be destroyed, and to have a united Ireland. Even if they were to join a government it's only until such time as they can destroy the government and the state.

(Ian Paisley, December 1981)

SOURCE 2 — Protestant suspicions

The more militant Protestants reached the stage by the end of 1971 in which they identified the whole Catholic community with the IRA.

(T. W. Moody, 'The Ulster Question', 1974)

Working-class Protestants celebrate the end of power-sharing. Why were they so pleased?

Then in May 1974 a group of working class Protestants, known as the Ulster Workers' Council, called a general strike. This aimed to bring the whole of Northern Ireland to a standstill and 'break' the Power Sharing Executive.

The Ulster Workers' Council strike began on May 14 1974. At first it was not taken seriously by very many people. On May 15 the Belfast correspondent of 'The Times' wrote,

'It seems likely that Belfast will suffer no more than a slight loss of power during the day-time hours.'

Two days later a British minister, Stan Orme, said,

'We're going to break this strike. I can tell you this — you're wasting your time. There is no question of negotiation with these bigots.'

But the strike soon became very serious. UDA road blocks paralysed Belfast; petrol and electricity were severely limited.

Blockade and march on Stormont, 1974.

By May 27 the strike had escalated even more. The strikers threatened a complete shut-down at the electricity power stations and sewage pumping stations. Faced with this awful prospect, Faulkner resigned on May 28 and the power-sharing Executive came to an end. For the first time in Irish or British history an administration had been brought down by a general strike.

Look at sources 3-5.

▶ *Why did the British government fail to break the strike as they hoped?*

▶ *How could events have worked out differently?*

SOURCE 3 — The part played by Protestant private armies

(A cartoon in F. Evans, 'Ireland for beginners', 1983)

What does this cartoon say about the treatment of Protestants who disagreed with the strike?

SOURCE 4 — The British Prime Minister's television message to the strikers

The people on this side of the water — British parents — have seen their sons spat upon and murdered. British taxpayers have seen the taxes they have poured out, almost without regard to cost, going into Northern Ireland. They see property destroyed by evil violence and are asked to pick up the bill for rebuilding it. Yet people who benefit from this now viciously defy Westminster, people who spend their lives sponging on Westminster and British democracy. Who do these people think they are?

(Harold Wilson, British Prime Minister, 25 May 1974)

Glen Barr of the UDA, one of the strike organisers.

SOURCE 5 — The impact of Wilson's speech

The UWC were delighted. Glen Barr, their leader, said later that they thought of making Wilson an 'honorary' member of the Ulster Workers' Council.

'Any hope he had of wrecking the strike went with that speech,' he said.

(Robert Fisk, 'The Point of No Return', 1976)

The hunger strikes 1981

When the IRA Provisionals appeared on the streets of Derry and Belfast in 1970 they said they had come to protect the Catholic community from Protestant violence. They got a mixed reception. Some Catholics did welcome them as protectors. Many merely tolerated the Provos because they were too afraid to do otherwise. Others, however, spoke out against violence of all kinds. By the end of 1970 a new peaceful Nationalist party had been formed — the SDLP. The SDLP were keen to find peaceful ways of sorting out differences with the Unionists. In 1976 two Catholics, Mairead Corrigan and Betty Williams, founded the Women's Peace Movement. Over the next two years they organised a series of peace marches which were supported by people on both sides. For a time there seemed a chance that the IRA would again be rejected by the Catholic community, as they had been during the 1956-62 bombing campaign.

Mairead Corrigan and the Peace Women 1976.

Then in 1981 a group of IRA prisoners began a hunger strike in the Maze prison (or H Blocks as they called it). The hunger strike was the climax of several years of prison protest in Northern Ireland. From the start of the recent Troubles, the Nationalist prisoners have insisted that they should not be treated like ordinary criminals. The British government agreed to their demands in 1972, and gave 'special category' privileges to prisoners who had committed crimes for political reasons. They were no longer forced to wear prison uniform or to do prison work.

In 1976 the British changed their policy and abolished the 'special category'. The IRA prisoners in the Maze Prison reacted to the changed rules by starting the 'blanket protest'. They refused to wear prison clothes and remained naked, except for blankets. In 1978 the prisoners stepped up their pressure by soiling their cells with their own excrement. The British refused to grant a return to special category, and in 1980 the IRA and INLA decided on a hunger strike. The first hunger strike ended in confusion in December, but on March 1 Bobby Sands began his fast. The British Prime Minister Margaret Thatcher insisted on not giving in to Sands and the other hunger strikers. By October ten men were dead and the hunger strike was called off.

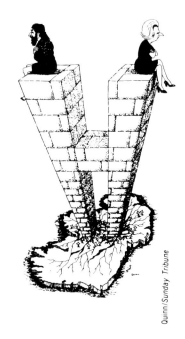

Quinn/Sunday Tribune

Margaret Thatcher and the 'H' block prison protest. What is this cartoon suggesting about Margaret Thatcher's attitude to the hunger strikes?

Look at sources 6-11.

▶ *Why did the British government refuse to give in to the demands of the hunger strikers?*

▶ *What was the effect of the hunger strikes on Northern Catholics?*

▶ *Was this what the hunger strikers intended?*

SOURCE 6 — Margaret Thatcher's reaction, March 1981

There is no such thing as political murder, political bombing or political violence. We will not compromise on this. There will be no political status.

SOURCE 7 — An IRA victory

Ten people had the courage to stand by their country to the point of dying for it. The H Block issue became a worldwide issue. The Republican movement gained enormously in the number of people who joined, in favourable publicity and in finance.

(Daithi O'Conaill, Sinn Fein December, 1981)

The hunger strike had a long tradition — the funeral of Nationalist hunger striker Terence MacSwiney, 1920.

The hunger strikes won great support among ordinary Catholics.

SOURCE 8 — The hunger strikes and Belfast Catholics

There were people on the marches against the government's treatment of the hunger strikers who had never been on a march before. Never was there such a determination among the mass of people to have done with the British government. It was now possible to speak respectfully of the IRA.

(Des Wilson, a Catholic priest from Belfast, October 1981)

SOURCE 9 — The thoughts of a peace campaigner

When Bobby Sands died many of us felt it's back to square one. If you tried to call a peace rally now you wouldn't get anyone to come. There is far more bitterness and a feeling of anti-Britishness.

(Mairead Corrigan, leader of the Women's Peace Movement, December 1981)

SOURCE 10 — A Protestant reaction

We were led to believe that only a minority of Catholics supported violence. To Protestants the hunger strike showed that Catholics were prepared to support the gunmen who murdered their fellow citizens.

(Frank Millar, Official Unionist Party, May 1983)

SOURCE 11 — The motives of Bobby Sands

He knows that if he dies, through his death, there will be so much anger stored up in the Irish people that it will fuel the struggle for the next ten years.

(Danny Morrison, Sinn Fein, March 1981)

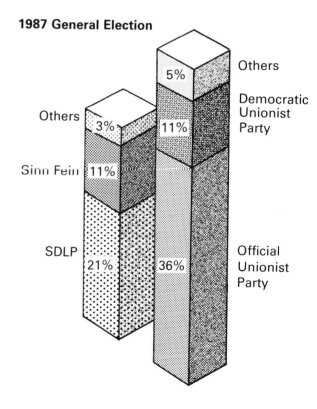

1987 General Election

The level of Catholic support for the hunger strikers and the IRA was shown to the whole world in May 1981 when over 50,000 people went to the funeral of Bobby Sands. Since then Sinn Fein has fought all major elections and had some success in winning votes from the SDLP.

▶ *How could events have worked out differently?*

The turning point that never was: Churchill offers a united Ireland, 1940

In the autumn of 1939 Britain went to war with Germany. By May 1940 the war was going badly and Chamberlain, the Prime Minister, resigned. He was replaced by Winston Churchill who eventually led Britain to victory. Churchill had long taken an interest in Irish politics, and in 1921 he had been involved in the Irish Treaty negotiations.

Churchill — the British wartime leader.

▶ *What was Churchill's attitude to the Northern Ireland question before the War?*

SOURCE 1 — A promise to the people of Northern Ireland

England will defend Ulster as if it were Kent or Lancashire. We could no more allow hostile hands to be laid upon the Protestant North than we could allow the Isle of Wight to fall into the hands of the Germans. Until Ulstermen wish to abandon the British Empire, the British Empire will never abandon them.

(Winston Churchill, 'The Daily Mail', February 1933)

During its very first days Churchill's government made an offer to the Dublin government that broke the promise of 1933. The following document was made public in 1980, forty years after it was drawn up.

SOURCE 2 — The 1940 offer of unification (made to Eamon de Valera on 28 June 1940)

(i) A declaration will be made by the UK Government immediately accepting the offer of a United Ireland. The declaration will give a solemn promise that the Union is to become at an early date an accomplished fact from which there shall be no turning back.

(ii) British naval vessels will have the use of ports in Eire and other British forces will be stationed in Eire.

(iii) The Government of Eire will arrest all Germans and Italians in the country.

(British government document of June 1940)

▶ *Why did Churchill make this extraordinary offer in 1940?*

Germany threatens Britain, June 1940.

Look at the problems he faced at the time.

SOURCE 3 — The early days of the Second World War

The war began disastrously for Britain and her allies. German square helmets became a familiar sight in Western Europe. The German forces poured across Holland, Belgium, Denmark and Norway. By May 1940 the British army were stranded in the Channel port of Dunkirk but, by an incredible feat, her shattered army was evacuated under the nose of the Germans. On 22 June 1940, France surrendered. Britain now stood alone. There was nothing to stop Hitler invading Britain except a handful of RAF fighters, a defeated army and badly equipped Home Guards.

(P. Darvill and W. Stirling, 'The Exploding Years', 1974)

A British comment on the refusal of Eire to join in the fight against Germany.

▶ *How did the Northern Ireland government respond to the British offer of unification?*

SOURCE 4 — The Northern Ireland Prime Minister replies to Churchill

AM PROFOUNDLY SHOCKED AND DISGUSTED BY YOUR LETTER MAKING SUGGESTIONS SO FAR REACHING BEHIND MY BACK AND WITHOUT ANY PRE-CONSULTATION WITH ME. TO SUCH TREACHERY TO LOYAL ULSTER I WILL NEVER BE A PARTY.

(Telegram sent by Lord Craigavon to the British government, 27 June 1940)

De Valera — the Irish Prime Minister.

Craigavon (formerly James Craig) the Prime Minister of Northern Ireland.

▶ *How did the South respond?*

If the Eire government in Dublin had accepted the British plan the history of Ireland could have been very different.

▶ *Can you suggest in what way?*

In fact de Valera said 'no' to the British offer. The reasons why he did so are complex. Look at sources 5 and 6.

▶ *What were his motives?*

Dunkirk — the British Army in retreat.

SOURCE 5 — de Valera replies to Churchill

We are unable to accept the plan. The plan would involve our entry into the war. Our people would be quite unprepared for it, and Dail Eireann (the Dublin parliament) would certainly reject it.

We are, of course, aware that a policy of neutrality has its dangers. But, on the other hand, our entry into the war would involve us in dangers greater still. The plan gives no guarantee that in the end we would have a united Ireland. Lord Craigavon could prevent unification by demanding concessions to which the majority of the Irish people could not agree.

(Eamon de Valera to the British government, 4 July 1940)

SOURCE 6 — de Valera's decision: a historian's view

He did undoubtedly believe that Craigavon would try to sabotage the plan for Irish unity. The British had gone back on their 1921 promise to negotiate the border in favour of the twenty-six counties. Could they be trusted to ensure Northern Ireland's co-operation in 1940, if necessary against the province's will? De Valera did not want a second generation of young Irishmen to die in another European war. It was scarcely ignoble of him to think that Britain was about to be defeated. If Britain had lost the war, Eire would inevitably have been occupied by German troops.

(Robert Fisk, 'In Time of War', 1983)

Ireland and the wider world

Because Ireland has been closely linked with Britain for so long, it would be easy to think that today's conflict is just another episode in British history. But for centuries there have been links between Ireland and other countries. In this section we shall be looking at some of these links and thinking about two key questions:

▶ *How have people in other countries influenced the conflict in Ireland?*
▶ *What impact has Ireland's conflict had on the wider world?*

Britain and her world empire

In the years from 1500-1914, many European countries built up overseas empires. By 1914 they controlled large areas of the world. The most powerful of these world empires was the British Empire. Ireland was part of Britain's empire for around 400 years. In fact, Ireland was one of Britain's first colonies, conquered at about the same time as the West Indies and parts of America. Britain's colonies were all different but they were important for one of two main reasons:

1   Economic reasons
Some colonies provided cheap food like tea and sugar for Britain's growing population and cheap raw materials like cotton for her developing industries. They also provided a market for British manufactured goods — woollens, cottons, metalware etc. The most important of these colonies were India and the West Indies.

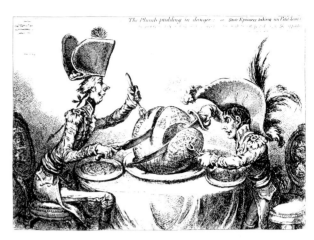

The plum pudding in danger. An English cartoon of the 18th century showing the world as a pudding being carved up by British and French leaders.

2   Strategic reasons
Other colonies were important because they protected Britain's sea routes across the world. These sea routes were Britain's lifeline. They brought the food and raw materials which made Britain the most powerful industrial and trading nation in the world. Two of the major strategic bases were Palestine and Aden.

The British Empire at the end of the 19th century.

Britain's global fears

1790-1800
Britain went to war with France after the French Revolution. Twice the French sent armies to Ireland, with Wolfe Tone, the Irish Nationalist. Both attacks ended disastrously.

1939-45 World War II
During World War II Britain feared that Hitler would use the South as a base to invade Ireland. British leaders made plans for a counter-attack from the North.

1914-18 World War I
During World War I, Germany hoped for a Nationalist rising in Ireland. They tried to land both arms and the Nationalist leader Roger Casement. The British captured the weapons and Casement.

1689-1691
With French backing the former King, James II went to Ireland, to try to win back his throne. James was a Catholic and hoped for support from Irish Catholics. France was at war with England and sent 7,000 soldiers to Ireland. The new King, William of Orange, defeated the French/Irish Catholic army at the Battle of the Boyne 1690.

1601
A Spanish army of 3,500 landed near Cork to join forces with Irish Catholic rebels. They were defeated by the English at Kinsale.

1579-80
Two small Italian armies landed in support of Irish Catholic rebels. They were financed by the Pope and the King of Spain who wished to destroy the English Queen, Elizabeth I.

Ireland and Britain's enemies, 1570s-1980s.

Ireland had a special strategic importance within the Empire because it was so close to Britain. At the closest point, only 12 miles separate Ireland and the rest of the UK. Ireland dominates the west coast of Britain and, as a powerful and aggressive country, Britain was certain to have enemies. Conflicts over the Empire and its colonies often led to war. Britain's enemies have usually been other European countries. For British governments, there was a constant threat that war would involve an enemy invasion and that Ireland could be used as a base for such an invasion. Their fears were confirmed by the fact that Britain's enemies tried many times to land troops in Ireland as a first step to conquering Britain.

Look at the map.

▶ *Which countries have been Britain's enemies?*

▶ *When and why did they try to use Ireland as a base for invasion?*

For over three hundred years Britain's enemies tried to use Ireland and Irish Catholics to destroy Britain. This affected Britain's attitude to Irish demands for independence in the 19th century.

SOURCE 1 — Ireland must be kept, 1872

Ireland must be kept, like India, at all costs; by persuasion if possible, if not by force.

(Lord Salisbury, Conservative politician, 1872)

▶ *How did this help to cause conflict in Ireland between 1870-1918?*

Britain and the South 1921-45

After British leaders finally gave independence to the South of Ireland in 1921, they remained worried about the threat to Britain's security. For this reason they kept control of three southern ports until 1937. When the Second World War broke out in 1939 the British feared that Hitler would invade Ireland as a first stage towards taking over Britain. Churchill, the British Prime Minister, tried to persuade Southern leaders to join the war on Britain's side by offering to reunite Ireland. De Valera refused this offer and insisted on staying out of the fighting.

▶ *Ulster Protestants did not find out about Churchill's offer until the 1980s. How do you think this news might have affected their attitude to Britain's recent talks with the Irish Republic?*

Britain and the North 1945 onwards

Since 1945 Southern leaders have refused to take sides in the 'Cold War' between Russia and other western countries, including Britain. Some people believe that this has made Britain more determined to hold onto Ulster as a strategic base.

SOURCE 2 — Part of Ireland must be kept, 1951

Throughout history Ireland, which has never been able to protect herself against invasion, has always been a potential base of attack on the United Kingdom. It is important that a part of that island should wish to remain part of the United Kingdom and its defence system.

(British Commonwealth Office, 1951)

SOURCE 3 — The British will hold on to Ulster, 1982

The Tories are obsessed by the Russian threat to Europe. This has made Britain conclude that she needs a strategic armed force in Ireland to guard the Atlantic sea routes to Britain.

(Daithi O'Connaill, Provisional Sinn Fein, 1982)

In 1983 Southern leaders told the British government that they would never allow their territory to be used as a base for attacks on Britain.

▶ *Why might Britain's policy have helped to cause conflict in the North in recent years?*
▶ *In an age of nuclear war and submarine-launched missiles, is Ireland still a threat to Britain's security?*

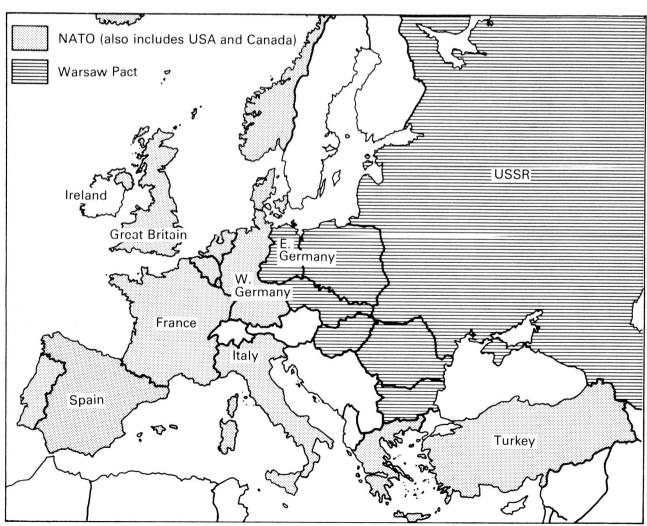

NATO (also includes USA and Canada)

Warsaw Pact

Ireland

Great Britain

France

Spain

Italy

E. Germany

W. Germany

USSR

Turkey

British and Irish

The British looked on the Empire as vitally important for their future as a rich and powerful nation. Many British settlers went out to the colonies, like the Protestants of the Ulster Plantation. Some organised loyal governments, others ran the plantations, mines and trading companies which supplied Britain's food and raw materials. But most of these colonies also had native people who had lived there long before the British arrived. How important were they to their British masters?

The British and their Irish colony

The native Irish people spoke a different language from their British rulers. Apart from this the British and the Irish had much in common.

Look at sources 4-9.
▶ *What did the British think of ordinary Irish people?*
▶ *What was their attitude to the Revolutionary Nationalists who opposed British rule?*
▶ *Have British attitudes changed since the break-up of the Empire?*
▶ *Can you suggest any reasons why the British felt this way about the Irish?*

SOURCE 4 — Why the Norman conquest would be good for the Irish

The Irish are wild, unfriendly people. They live like beasts. They grow little food in their fields. The soil is not to blame but the laziness of the people. Above all people, they cannot be trusted. When they give their word to anyone, they do not keep it. Their beards, clothes and minds are so barbarous that they cannot be said to have any culture.

(Giraldus Cambrensis, 'History and Topography of Ireland', written after visits in 1183 and 1185)

SOURCE 5 — An English novelist describes the Irish, 1860

I am haunted by the human chimpanzees I saw along that hundred miles of horrible country. I don't believe they are our fault. I believe there are not only more of them than of old, but that they are happier, better, more comfortably fed and lodged under our rule than they ever were. But to see white chimpanzees is dreadful; if they were black one would not feel it so much.

(Charles Kingsley in a letter to his wife, July 1860)

SOURCE 6 — An 'Irish joke' from the 1980s

Paddy: 'What happens if this bomb goes off in the car?'
Mick: 'It's alright — there's another one in the boot.'

SOURCE 7 — A British view of the IRB, 1882

The IRB men had just murdered the British Chief Secretary to Ireland in Dublin.

SOURCE 8 — A British view of the IRA, 1978

The IRA are not soldiers fighting a war but sneak killers with personality problems.

('Daily Express', December 1978)

SOURCE 9 — A British view of the IRA, 1974

('The Spectator', 1974)

SOURCE 10 — Comments after a visit to Ulster, July 1970

For God's sake bring me a large scotch (whisky). What a bloody awful country.

(Reginald Maudling, British Home Secretary, 1970)

The Irish and their British masters

British attitudes produced a strong reaction from most Irish people.

Look at sources 1-5.
▶ *What did the Revolutionary Nationalists think of their British rulers?*
▶ *Have their views changed since the break up of the Empire?*
▶ *How do you think these views have helped to cause today's conflict in Ireland?*

SOURCE 1 — An Irish cartoon showing the wicked British jailer keeping sweet Erin (Ireland) imprisoned

(From 'Weekly Freeman', 23 May 1885)

SOURCE 2 — Beware the British, 1915

Consider what this British Empire is doing. Everywhere it holds down races so that it can prevent them developing their own economies and force them to remain customers of British produce. To do this it stifles India, smothers South Africa and plans the partition of Ireland.

(James Connolly, a Revolutionary Nationalist and a leading figure in the 1916 Easter Rising)

SOURCE 3 — 'The Execution of soldier Mountbatten', 1979

In claiming responsibility for the death of Lord Mountbatten (former chief of the UK defence staff, cousin of the Queen of England and symbol of all that is imperial Britain) the Provisional IRA stated that the bombing was:

'To bring to the attention of the English people the continuing occupation of our country. The British government continue with the oppression of our people. Well for this we will tear out their imperialist heart.'

(Report from 'Republican News', September 1979)

SOURCE 4 — Terrorists or freedom fighters? 1985

We are here to honour the freedom fighters of the IRA.

(Martin McGuinness, speaking at the 1985 commemoration of the 1916 Easter Rising)

SOURCE 5 — Graffiti on a wall in 1977 — the year of the Queen's Silver Jubilee

Britain's other colonies

SOURCE 6 — Thoughts of a British Empire builder in Africa, 1890s

We, (the British) are the finest race in the world and the more of the world we inhabit the better it is for the human race. Just fancy those parts that are at present inhabited by the most despicable specimens of human beings.

(Cecil Rhodes, who became Premier of Cape Colony in South Africa, 1890)

SOURCE 7 — British settlers and American Indians, 1790s

Instead of respecting the rights of the Indians as an independent nation, they looked on them as wild animals that ought to be banished from the face of the earth. Instead of keeping to their own land, they fixed themselves in the land of the Indians without their consent.

(Isaac Weld, English traveller, 1790s)

SOURCE 8 — The British and the Palestinian Arabs, 1919

In Palestine we do not propose even to consult the wishes of the 700,000 Arabs who now inhabit that ancient land.

(Lord Balfour, British Foreign Secretary, 1919)

SOURCE 9 — The British in India, 1890s

Even the most scrubby, mean Englishman regards himself as infinitely superior to an Indian with a family tree going back 1000 years.

(A comment in 'The Times' in the 1890s)

Look at sources 6-9.
▶ *In what ways were British attitudes to other native people similar to their attitude to the Irish?*
▶ *What do you think these people thought of the British?*

THE RHODES COLOSSUS
STRIDING FROM CAPE TOWN TO CAIRO.

A British cartoon referring to Cecil Rhodes' plans for a British take-over of Africa in the 1890s.

Guerrillas, terrorists and freedom fighters

The English have always looked on Ireland's Revolutionary Nationalists as 'terrorists'. The Revolutionaries, on the other hand, have always seen themselves as 'freedom fighters'.

These two different words used to describe people who try to overthrow governments and bring about revolutions using the cannon, the gun or the bomb. The word you choose depends to some extent on which side you support.

For the last 200 years Irish Nationalists have looked for ideas and support to foreign revolutionaries. These were people seen by the Irish as fellow freedom fighters.

Look at the chart opposite.

▶ *When and how have foreign revolutionaries become involved in the conflict in Ireland?*
▶ *Why do you think the French were so keen to help Irish Revolutionary Nationalists?*
▶ *Why have the Irish Revolutionaries had help from Libya and the PLO?*

The French Revolution 1789

In 1789 the French people overthrew their government and set up a parliament for all the people. Wolfe Tone and Irish Nationalists were very impressed by the French revolution.

'We knew what it was to be enslaved. We want equal representation of all people in Parliament' (Wolfe Tone).

In 1795 the new Revolutionary government in France issued a 'Decree of Armed Propaganda'. This offered help to all peoples who want to recover their freedom . . . Wolfe Tone asked for armed French soldiers to attack the British in Ireland.

The Palestine Liberation Organisation (PLO) 1970s and 80s

Between 1918-48 Palestine was a British military base. During this time, the British allowed thousands of European Jews to settle there against the wishes of the native Palestinian Arabs. After 1948 Jews and Arabs fought a bitter war for control of Palestine. The Jews took control of large areas of Palestinian land and set up their own state of Israel. Thousands of Palestinians became stateless refugees. Since 1964 Palestinian Nationalists of the PLO have been fighting to regain their homeland. They blame the British for allowing Jewish settlers into Palestine. Because of this they have been sympathetic towards the IRA and their 'struggle for freedom'.

'45 IRA men found shelter with the PLO. Thomas MacMahon, convicted for the murder of Lord Mountbatten in 1979, was trained in a PLO camp' (adapted from 'The PLO' by Jill Becker, 1984)

A long line of Irish revolutionaries

1798 Wolfe Tone and the United Irishmen rise in armed revolt.

1800

1848 Young Irelanders revolt against British forces in Ireland.

1850

1867 The Fenian revolt in Ireland organised by IRB (Irish Republican Brotherhood).

1900

1916 IRB organise the Easter Rising — an armed rebellion in Dublin.

1919 The Irish revolution and War of Independence.
–21 IRB volunteers become IRA (Irish Republican Army).

1969 The Provisional IRA begins attacks on the
–70 British Army in Ulster.

1980

The British-American revolution 1775-83

In 1775 the British colonists in America began a long War of Independence to free themselves from the British King and Empire. In 1776, they drew up their Declaration of Independence.

The ideas of the American colonists inspired Wolfe Tone to rebel against British rule.

The Irish-American revolutionaries

In the 19th century thousands of Irish people emigrated to America especially after the Great Famine in 1845. They carried with them strong anti-British feelings. In 1858 the Fenian Brotherhood was set up, dedicated to a violent overthrow of British rule in Ireland. Since then, Irish Americans have continued to send money and guns to support Revolutionary Nationalists in Ireland.

The Libyan connection

Libya is an Arab country in North Africa. During World War II the British army held Libya as a military base. In 1953 a pro-British King, Idris, was put in power. His government was corrupt and relied on the rent paid by Britain for its military bases. In 1969 King Idris was overthrown by Arab Nationalists led by Colonel Gaddafi. Gaddafi has been accused of supplying arms to the IRA.

'These bombs which are convulsing Britain and breaking its spirit are the bombs of the Libyan people. We have sent them to the Irish revolutionaries so that the British will pay the price for their past misdeeds'.
(Libyan newspaper, 1981)

IRA guerrillas show the way

After 1921 the Irish revolutionaries had an influence on Nationalists in other countries. Between 1919-21, Irish Nationalists fought a guerrilla war against the British. This was not an open war with battle lines of uniformed soldiers but a 'secret' war of sabotage and surprise attacks. As we have seen, the Irish Nationalists won. Although they had not beaten the British army in battle, the Nationalists had broken the will of the government to carry on fighting.

SOURCE 1 — The price of resisting was too high

The price of resisting the Nationalists was too high — both in money and embarrassment to ministers caught out by questions in parliament about British brutality. Rather than order another Black and Tans operation, the government decided they would bend before the winds of nationalism.

(Brian Lapping, 'End of Empire', 1985)

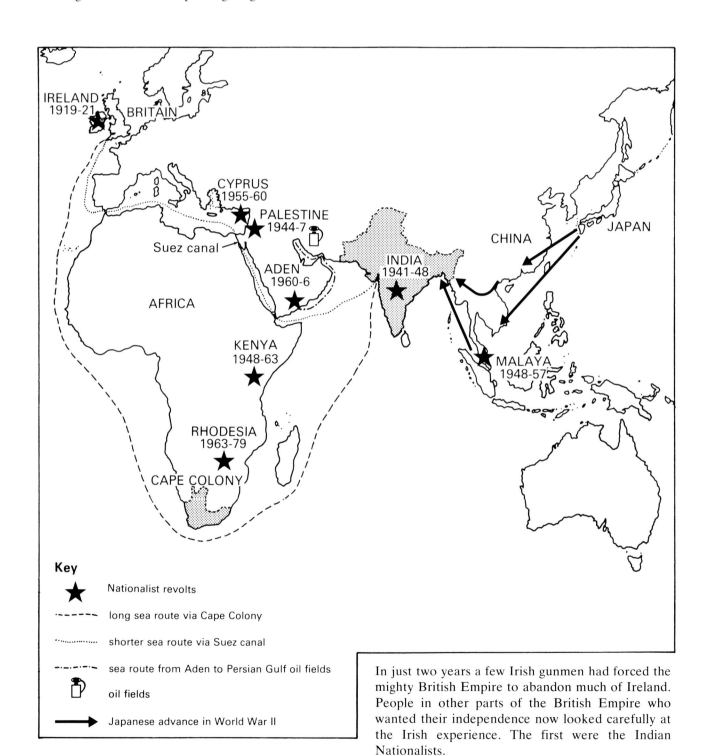

Key

★ Nationalist revolts

------ long sea route via Cape Colony

.... shorter sea route via Suez canal

—·—·— sea route from Aden to Persian Gulf oil fields

🛢 oil fields

➤ Japanese advance in World War II

In just two years a few Irish gunmen had forced the mighty British Empire to abandon much of Ireland. People in other parts of the British Empire who wanted their independence now looked carefully at the Irish experience. The first were the Indian Nationalists.

Nationalist revolts in British colonies after 1900.

Indian Nationalists and the IRA

India was the most important colony in the British Empire. At first it was important for trade. By 1914 it was important for *men* and *money*. In the two World Wars India sent *and paid for* 3 million men to fight for Britain. As one historian put it:

'India provided the muscle of the British Empire: it was like a gigantic engine of war'.

Indian Nationalists had begun to demand 'Home Rule' for their country in the 1880s. Like the Irish Nationalists, some wanted to win independence by peaceful persuasion. Others believed that only violence would make the British leave India.

After the 1914-18 War, Nationalist leaders organised a massive campaign of civil disobedience (peaceful non-cooperation with their British rulers). The British eventually promised independence but without setting a date. When World War II began in 1939, the British needed India more than ever. Some Nationalists decided that the only way to get rid of the British was to side with her enemies. Led by Subhas Chandra Bose, they set up the Indian National Army (INA) to fight alongside the Japanese.

Armed Indian nationalists during the Second World War.

SOURCE 2 — An Indian Nationalist looks to the IRA

In the history of our fight against British imperialists, there is no other struggle which has influenced us so much, and for which we have so much sympathy, as that of the brave Irish nation.

(Subhas Chandra Bose, founder of the INA, 1944)

Again the British decided that the price of resisting was too high. They finally gave India its independence three years after the War, in 1948.

▶ *How many similarities can you spot between the Indian and the Irish struggles for independence?*

The spread of guerrilla wars

After the Second World War other parts of the British Empire began to fight for their independence. They also tried to learn from the success of the IRA in 1919-21. In Palestine, Cyprus and Aden, the Nationalists followed a policy of regularly killing British troops and police. In each of these places the British eventually agreed to pull out — not because they were defeated, but because the government and public opinion were sick of the British deaths.

British troops leaving Aden.

Algerian nationalists caused similar problems for the French in the 1950s. French public opinion grew tired of the struggle, and the French pulled out of Algeria in 1962. A guerrilla war by Vietnamese communists forced the powerful American Army to retreat from Vietnam in 1973. Again the vital factor was that people were sickened by seeing their own men die.

▶ *Many anti-British nationalist groups learned from the success of the IRA in 1921. Does this mean that the IRA was a major cause of the break up of the British Empire?*

A network of terror?

Since 1968 there has been a great rise in the number of revolutionary groups across the world. Some of the groups accused of terrorism have links with the IRA. For example, an organisation called ETA wants the Basque people, who live in Northern Spain, to break away from Spain and form a separate country. ETA has consistently used bombing and murder to force the Spanish government to give them what they want. In December 1973 ETA blew up the Prime Minister, Luis Carrero Blanco, and the Spanish government accused the IRA of supplying the explosives.

Today's Provisional IRA has returned to the guerrilla tactics of 1919-21. The Provisionals hope to so sicken the British people that the government is forced to withdraw the army from Ulster.

▶ *Many people argue that the recent IRA campaign has been counter-productive. (That means it has had the opposite effect to that intended.) What do they mean? Are they right?*

The Irish-American connection

Poverty and the threat of starvation drove millions of Irish people to emigrate during the 19th century. The heaviest period of emigration came during and immediately after the Great Famine 1845-49. The population of Ireland fell dramatically from 8 million in 1841 to 4½ million in 1901.

The emigrants went to many places across the world carrying with them strong anti-British feelings. the most popular destination was the USA; by 1870 there were nearly 2 million Irish-born people living in America. Ever since the Famine and the emigration, some Irish-Americans have consistently supported the idea of driving the British out of Ireland by force.

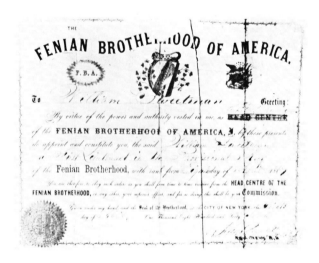

An American Fenian certificate of the 1860s. Since the famine violent Nationalism has always had Irish-American supporters.

Fenians and Clan-na-Gael

The Irish Republican Brotherhood (The Fenians) was founded in America in 1858. It was dedicated to a violent overthrow of British rule in Ireland. Hundreds of Irish-Americans returned home, to take part in the disastrous Fenish Rising of 1867. Despite this failure, the Fenians remained strong in America. In the 1870s, a Fenian, John Devoy, set up a new Irish-American organisation. This was called Clan-na-Gael and it raised money in the USA for Irish nationalists. In 1880 Clan-na-Gael organised a trip to America for Parnell, during which he collected £200,000.

Irish-Americans and the Easter Rising 1916

Both the IRB and Clan-na-Gael took part in the planning of the Easter Rising. One member, Tom Clarke, returned from New York in 1907 specifically to help organise a rebellion.

The Easter Rising had a great effect on Irish-Americans.

Noraid 1970s-1980s

Some Irish-Americans have continued to send help to the IRA, from its formation after the Easter Rising, right up to the present day. Support for the Provisional IRA has been organised since 1969 by a group known as **Noraid.** It is estimated that Noraid raised £4 million for the Provisionals between 1970 and 1982. Members of Noraid have admitted smuggling arms to Northern Ireland.

Irish Americans often demonstrate against British policy in Ireland.

The Widow Makers

American supporters provide most of the arms for the Provisional IRA today. The American Armalite rifle is their most important weapon.

The American Armalite — a favourite weapon of the IRA.

SOURCE 3 — The 'widow-maker'

The Armalite or 'widow maker' has played an important role in IRA successes since 1969. It is supplied to the US army as the M16 and can pierce a flak jacket at 500 yards. But it is the sporting version. the Armalite AR15, which has reached Ulster in bulk. Weighing only 7lb, it can be dismantled into several pieces; brought to a hideout by five or six women, assembled, fired and rapidly spirited away in handbags or pockets. It has proved ideal for the urban guerrilla and 'single-shot sniper' in Ulster. 80% of Armalites there have proved to be of US origin.

(Adapted from an article by Godfrey Barker in 'The Spectator', November 1975)

American Armalites were amongst the massive consignment of weapons that was seized by the Irish navy in September 1984. The arms were on board a fishing vessel, the 'Marita Anne' and they had been bought in the USA, probably with Noraid money.

Young Irish Americans — memories of the old country and anti-British ideas are passed on to each new generation.

American politicians and Ireland

John Hume of the SDLP has been responsible for getting the support of American politicians, including some who are not Irish-American. He hoped that the American government would put pressure on Britain to make changes in Northern Ireland. Charles Haughey of Fianna Fail has also tried to get America to push for Irish unity.

In the 1970s President Carter seemed willing to get involved in negotiating an Irish settlement. Not all Irish-Americans support the IRA, however. A group of senior politicians, led by Senator Edward Kennedy, have condemned the Provisionals and asked their fellow Irish-Americans to stop helping them. At the same time Kennedy believes that the British are partly to blame and should work towards getting out of Northern Ireland.

President Reagan has made it clear that he wants nothing to do with the argument over Irish unity. In 1981 Reagan ignored a request from Dublin that he should intervene in the hunger strikes.

Explaining motives

The families of today's Irish-Americans have, in many cases, been in America for much more than a century.

▶ Why do you think they are still so strong in their support for Irish nationalism?
▶ Why do you think some of them are stronger supporters of the IRA than most Catholics actually living in Ireland?

What Next In Ireland?

New political moves

The British have had an 'Irish Problem' and the Irish a 'British Problem' for over 400 years. During that time the following political ways of solving the problem have been tried:

1. Complete control of all Ireland by the British.
2. Northern Ireland part of the UK, but with its own Parliament for internal affairs. Independence for the rest of Ireland.
3. Northern Ireland ruled directly from Britain. Independence for the rest of Ireland.
4. Northern Ireland ruled as part of UK, but with power sharing. Independence for the rest of Ireland.

Look back at pages 4-35.

▶ *When was each of these tried? Why did each fail?*

Solving old problems

Politics is only one of the long-term causes of the conflict in Ireland. One solution of the problem might be that the other long-term cause might die away — or changes could be made to help to get rid of them.

▶ *What might be done to solve the problems shown?*

Some people argue that the political problem has to be solved before the others can be tackled effectively. Some argue that the other problems must be solved first.

▶ *Use your knowledge of the history of the conflict in Ireland to decide which, if either, of these views is correct.*

There are other possible political solutions that have not been tried:

5. Complete control of all Ireland by a Dublin Government.
6. Northern Ireland to be a completely separate country independent of Britain and of the Republic.
7. The separate regions of Ireland could have their own local governments with a central government for matters concerning the whole country.
8. England, Northern Ireland, Wales, Scotland, and the Irish Republic all to be states in a 'United States of Europe'.
9. Northern Ireland to be run jointly by the British and Irish governments.

▶ *Use your historical knowledge to decide whether any of these solutions (or others you may think of) are likely or unlikely to succeed.*

What might be done to solve the problems of:
religion?
economics?
social conflict?

'Irish History is something which no Englishman should forget, and which no Irishman should remember.' G. B. Shaw, who wrote this, meant that the British should remember how unfairly Ireland had been treated in the past, and that the Irish should try to forget it. Perhaps instead of just remembering or forgetting history people should try to understand it.

▶ *How could understanding history help us to solve the conflict in Ireland?*

Understanding other modern world problems

The situation in Ireland is unique. No other conflict is **exactly** the same. But this does not mean that there aren't **similar** conflicts in other countries. You may find this idea difficult but just think about yourself. You are unique. No one else is exactly like you. Yet there are lots of other people who live in a similar way and face the same kind of problems.

Making sense of the conflict in Ireland may help us to understand other news stories about other conflicts elsewhere in the world.

You have to begin by asking the same questions about:

— the **causes** of the conflict
— the **motives** of the people involved

You have already read about the conflict in Palestine in the 1940s. Today there is still fighting between Jews and Palestinian Arabs, both in Israel and other countries.

Look at the pictures below relating to the conflict between Jews and Arabs.

▶ *Can you spot any similarities between this conflict and the troubles in Ireland?*

A demonstration outside the Israeli Embassy in London, 1973.

How far back do the causes go?
Do things always work out as intended?
Were there turning points when things might have worked out differently?
Was there one cause or many?
Are there just two sides or are there 'outsiders' involved?

Conflict between Jews and Arabs.
Are there any similarities with the conflict in Ireland?

Who's who in Ulster today

NATIONALIST/CATHOLIC

Political Groups

SDLP   **Social Democratic & Labour Party**
- started in 1970
- mainly Catholic
- wants to use peaceful, democratic means to get a united Ireland
- fiercely opposed to IRA violence

PSF   **Provisional Sinn Fein**
- a legal political party which supports the IRA in its campaign of violence
- since the 1980s it has put up candidates for local and national elections in the North

WP   **The Workers Party**
- a Nationalist party once linked to the IRA
- supports socialist idea eg. the reorganisation of industry so that it is controlled by the workers

Private Armies

IRA   **Irish Republican Army**
- has fought against the British in Ireland since 1919
- split in December 1969 into 'Official' and 'Provisional' IRA

IRA   **(Officials)**
- moved away from violent methods in early 1970s

IRA   **(Provisionals)**
- seen by British army as the main 'terrorist' group in Northern Ireland
- aims to force British out of Ulster 'by armed struggle'
- illegal in UK and the Republic of Ireland

INLA   **Irish National Liberation Army**
- formed in mid 1970s
- another breakaway group of IRA men
- small but ruthless private army
- has links with international 'terrorist' groups
- illegal but has a political front organisation — Irish Republican Socialist party

THE MIDDLE GROUND

Political Groups

ALL   **Alliance Party**
- founded in 1970
- has members from both sides
- aims to bring members from Catholic and Protestant communities together

Security Forces

British Regular Army
- sent to Ulster in 1969 as a peace keeping force with control over police until 1977
- since 1972 its numbers have been reduced

RUC — **Royal Ulster Constabulary**
- under army control 1969-77, since then had taken charge of security operations
- only 10% of its police are Catholic

UDR — **Ulster Defence Regiment**
- set up in 1970 after Protestant B Specials were disbanded
- recruits locally from Ulster Protestants and Catholics but today only 3% of its men are Catholics
- has some full time soldiers but relies mainly on part-timers
- supports RUC and Regular Army but not allowed to work in trouble spots eg. riots, staunchly Catholic areas of Derry and Belfast unless commanded by regular army officers

UNIONIST/PROTESTANT

Political Groups

OUP — **Official Unionist Party**
- formerly the Ulster Unionist Party — first set up in 1880s
- main Protestant political party until 1970-1

DUP — **Democratic Unionist Party**
- founded by Ian Paisley in 1971
- won backing of many Protestants who were unhappy with the OUP
- tough and uncompromising stand on keeping links with UK
- has taken much working class support away from OUP

Orange Order
- largest Protestant organisation in N. Ireland
- formed in 1795 to help protect Protestants
- still holds marches to celebrate the victory of William of Orange
- Orangemen are sworn to defend the Protestant religion
- they also support the OUP — though they are not a political party

Private Armies

UDA — **Ulster Defence Association**
- largest Protestant private army
- started in 1971
- supports the idea of an independent N. Ireland free of ties with UK and the Irish Republic

UVF — **Ulster Volunteer Force**

UFF — **Ulster Freedom fighters**
- two illegal Protestant paramilitary groups

INDEX

Acknowledgements

The author and the publisher acknowledge the following illustration sources. They have made every effort to trace the copyright holders but where they have failed, they will be happy to make the necessary arrangements at the first opportunity.

We are grateful to the following for permission to reproduce illustrations:

Associated Press   74 (right)
Belfast Telegraph   53 (middle)
BBC Hulton   11 21, 28 (top, middle and bottom), 58 (top), 68, 71 (bottom), 73 (left), 81 (left), 84 (left), 85 (bottom right), 96-97 (bottom), 99 (left)
British Library   5 (top left), 14 (bottom left)
Camera Press   53 (bottom), 76, 79 (bottom)
Century Newspapers   75 (top right)
Crawford Municipal Art Gallery   26 (top)
G. A. Duncan   29 (top right)
Mary Evans Picture Library   12 (right), 86 (top)
Fotomas Index   5 (middle left), 15, 43 (top right), 45
Free Palestine Information Office   99 (top right)
Stanley Gibbons   29 (bottom left)
Guardian   35, 38 (foot), 40 (top)
Horner/New Statesman   74 (left)
Illustrated London News   71 (top)
Imperial War Museum   25 (bottom left), 72 (right)
Irish Times   100
Mansell Collection   46 (top), 86 (bottom), 91, 93
Military Archive and Research Service   97 (top left)
National Library of Ireland   4 (top right), 16 (top), 17 (right), 24 (bottom), 54 (left), 56 (right), 67, 72 (bottom left), 82 (bottom), 89 (top), 90 (top)
National Museum of Ireland   56 (left), 64 (right), 66
Pacemaker Press   37 (top), 38 (top), 39 (bottom), 40 (bottom), 47 (bottom), 51, 52 (foot), 61 (top right), 78 (bottom), 79 (top), 80, 81 (bottom right), 83 (top)
Parker Gallery   17 (left)
Photo Source   4 (top left)
Popperfoto   5 (top right and bottom left), 34 (top), 37 (middle), 39 (top), 41 (top and bottom), 58 (bottom), 69 (top left and right), 72 (top), 78 (top), 82 (middle left), 85 (top right), 85 (bottom left), 95 (top)
Punch   70 (middle)
Quinn/Sunday Tribune   82 (top right)
Socialist Challenge   78 (middle)
Source Photographic Library   4 (bottom)
Spectator   89 (bottom)
Syndication International   34 (middle left), 100-101 (bottom)
Topham   64 (left), 69 (middle)
Topix   75 (bottom right), 77
Trinity College, Dublin   12 (left), 13 (right)
Ulster Folk and Transport Museum   50 (right)
Ulster Museum   5 (bottom right), 23 (top and bottom), 52 (top), 57, 61 (top left), 65
Weidenfeld & Nicholson Archives   14 (bottom left)
Liam White   97 (top right)
Writers and Readers Publishing Cooperative   38 (middle), 60 (left), 75 (top left), 75 (bottom right), 81 (top right)